NIGERIA, LEADERSHIP AND DEVELOPMENT: ESSAYS IN HONOUR OF CHIBUIKE ROTIMI AMAECHI.

EME N.EKEKWE

authorHOUSE®

AuthorHouse™ UK Ltd.
500 Avebury Boulevard
Central Milton Keynes, MK9 2BE
www.authorhouse.co.uk
Phone: 08001974150

First published by AuthorHouse   08/03/2011

ISBN: 978-1-4567-7773-9 (sc)
ISBN: 978-1-4567-7774-6 (hc)
ISBN: 978-1-4567-7775-3 (ebk)

Contents

DEDICATION

To Chinua Achebe, Wole Soyinka and all those Nigerians who refuse to accept mediocrity as the standard for this country.

ACKNOWLEDGMENT

The idea of this book was not conceived in the abstract. It was inspired by what appears to be a welcome departure in the way "business-as-usual" Nigeria leaders have gone about their supposed leadership role. The 2007 elections were thoroughly disappointing but even out of them there emerged a few governors who decided to set a different pace. The ones that struck one at the time were Babatunde Fashola of Lagos State and Chibuike Rotimi Amaechi of Rivers State. These were by no means revolutionary leaders but most residents in their States would readily acknowledge that they departed from the depressing norm. It was easy to see why the resulting essays should be in honour of Governor Amaechi: he started virtually from scratch whereas Governor Fashola appeared to have inherited something to build on. There is an Igbo proverb that says if one encourages the woman preparing the beans she would do even better. It is in that spirit that I acknowledge these and other gentlemen who stand up as signposts to good leadership in Nigeria.

In the course of preparing this work, I had cause to deny my nieces and nephews several opportunities of their favourite pastime of going with me to "give food to the fish" as the 'the Doc' among them would put it. If this work, in any way imaginable, helps to inspire the evolution of genuine leaders then the denial these promising suffered would have been worth the while. Only time will tell if Chibuihe, Jenny, Chibuzo, Grace, Chibuike, Nwachukwu, Joseph, Eme Ekekwe II and Eme Uwakwe will agree that it was better to have denied them their fishing rights than not follow through on this project.

Kelechi Samuel, CEO, Paperworks Limited, and Barrister Iche Wordu deserve my full appreciation for all the encouragement and support they gave generously in the course of doing this work.

Finally, undertaking an assignment of this nature can only be easy if one had the confidence of all the contributors. I enjoyed this in full measure. It seemed not to have mattered that some were already working under tight deadlines on other projects, they joyfully delivered on time. To all who in one way or another gave me their support I say, "a thousand thanks!" for making my work easy.

ABOUT THE BOOK

This book, *Nigeria, Leadership And Development: essays In Honour Of Chibuike Rotimi Amaechi. - Essays in Honour of Chibuike Rotimi Amaechi,* is an attempt to clarify the issue of leadership and how, in our circumstances, it has impeded (or for those who believe differently, facilitated) the achievement of the Nigeria project.

The philosophy behind this book is that if those who are doing well receive encouragement, they will see the need to remain focused and will stay the course. They may then inspire and attract others who may aim to achieve even more. It is always useful to be critical in evaluating those who lead, because it might help them to improve. But it is most unhelpful to always condemn everything and thus attract into the ring those who are entirely shameless. There is something to be gained by encouraging those who show signs of understanding that Nigeria cannot afford to continue muddling through, unless it wants to fall off the map in a globalized world. Leadership is an honour and an opportunity for service to humanity and not just a platform for self-promotion.

PETER EKEKWE
Executive Director
GARDENCITY LEADERSHIP INITIATIVE
Port Harcourt, Nigeria

ABOUT THE CONTRIBUTORS

Julius O. Ihonvbere, BA (Combined Honours) - History and Political Science (University of Ife, now Obafemi Awolowo University); MA - International Affairs (Carleton University); and PhD - Political Science (University of Toronto). He is a teacher, an administrator, a human rights and pro-democracy activist, a politician, an international scholar, and a consultant. He has authored over a dozen academic books and monographs and over 100 research and policy papers. Professor Ihonvbere was the project director of the Constitutionalism Project, International League for Human Rights, New York. He is the winner of the first Mario Zamora memorial award from the Association of Third World Studies in recognition of his academic and research work on developing nations, and an Officer of the Order of the Niger (OON).

Nimi Wariboko, BSc – (Economics, First Class Honours), Univ. of Port Harcourt; MBA (Finance/Accounting), Columbia University; MDiv, Oral Roberts University; and PhD (*summa cum laude*), Princeton. He is the Katherine B. Stuart Professor of Christian Ethics and has written extensively on social ethics, accounting, finance, management, economics, and political science. His latest book (2010) is *Ethics and Time: Ethos of Temporal Orientation in Politics and Religion of the Niger Delta*. He has taught at New York University and at the Frank G. Zarb School of Business, Hofstra University. This strategy consultant to top investment banks also has expertise in corporate financial analysis and is doing much to promote knowledge of Kalabari culture.

John Boye Ejobowah is associate professor in the Department of Global Studies, Wilfrid Laurier University, Waterloo, Ontario, Canada. He holds BSc and MSc in political science from the University of Port Harcourt, and a PhD also in political science from the University of Toronto. He previously taught at the University of Port Harcourt and at the University of Toronto. Ejobowah's work makes normative judgment of group claims to equality and of institutional arrangements for responding to such claims. He is the author of *Competing Claims to Recognition on the Nigerian Public Sphere*. Some of his other recent publications include chapters in *Assessing Territorial Pluralism, Ethnicity and Politics in Africa*, and in *Constitutional Design for Divided Societies: Integration or Accommodation?* as well as articles in such journals as *Commonwealth and Comparative Politics, Regional and Federal Studies*, and the *Canadian Journal of African Studies*.

Eme N. Ekekwe, BA (Hons.) in Political Science (Western Ontario); MA, PhD (Carleton) also in Political Science. He is a senior lecturer at the Department of Political and Administrative Studies, University of Port Harcourt. His research work and publications have been mainly in the areas of political theory and political economy. Ekekwe is the author of *Class and State in Nigeria* and *An Introduction to Political Economy*, as well as several monographs. He has experience in journalism, the public service, and the private sector. Eme Ekekwe has served in the federal government's Bitumen Project Implementation Committee (BPIC) and is currently the assistant director of the Emerald Institute for Energy Economics, Policy and Strategic Studies, University of Port Harcourt.

Nekabari Johnson Nna holds BSc and PhD degrees in Political Science from the University of Port Harcourt. He is currently a senior lecturer in the Department of Political and Administrative Studies, University of Port Harcourt. He is the author of several books, monographs, and chapters in books. His research interests include indigenous peoples/ human rights, comparative poverty, conflict studies, and sustainable development.

FOREWORD

Reflecting on my invitation to write the foreword to this collection of essays in honour of Governor Chibuike Rotimi Amaechi, I could not but recall my days with the then radical student activist/leader at the University of Port Harcourt and all our attempts to ensure that things changed for the better for the student population in general.

We would start with dialogue and with engagement of the school authorities, who, in their "bourgeois" (in this context, meaning "oppressor") attitude, would not yield an inch. This would naturally lead to strong agitation and protests, which we would then justify with a philosophical quote like "He who makes peaceful change impossible, makes violent change inevitable".

I still remember "Rotimi" addressing students, who had just been dispersed by the tear gas of "rioting" policemen, and quoting one of his favourite authors (I believe it was Franz Fanon) thus: "When you drive people from the arena where opinions are expressed, they only go to converge at the cellar where revolutions are born". That was Rotimi Chibuike Amaechi before he committed "class suicide".

So, it was no surprise that he made his way into politics, first as special assistant to the then deputy governor of Rivers State and, later, as Speaker of the Rivers State House of Assembly, before finally emerging as Governor of the State.

As he ventured into the murky waters of politics, I had quite a number of apprehensions. My concerns then, as indeed they have remained over the years, revolved largely around the challenges of governance in an under-developed economy. In the light of the obvious failures of the post-independence Nigerian state to minister to the basic needs of its people, was leadership at the sub-national level a calling to wish on one's worst foe?

Conversely, the litany of unfulfilled expectations that describe the five decades of this country's independence demand quality intervention at critical junctions of our national life. To paraphrase Ekekwe ("The Nigerian Leadership Question"), the country cannot continue to rely "for its economic and political survival mainly on crude oil".

The development challenges that confront us as a people clearly call for a select group who can summarily resolve the sundry dilemmas posed by our own Gordian knots. If this is not a requisition for leadership at all levels of our national life, then what is it? Caught between the Scylla of worrying for one's friend whose decision to take up political office might demand too much of him, and the Charybdis of concern for a nation whose perennial drift is increasingly accounted for by a failure of cross-sectoral leadership, I plumped several years ago for the latter.

At a much broader level, Professor Ihonvbere's chapter, "Leadership and Good Governance in Nigeria", speaks to what were then my biggest fears. In the vast emptiness that has come to describe our people's lack of access to piped water, health services, affordable schools, etc., a surfeit of "impunity, the abuse of office, rascality, and indiscipline" are complicit. There are a few commentators who blame these ills on the absence of accountability across every department of national life.

Nonetheless, while the nature and quality of representation is crucial to any meaningful definition of "governance", it is impossible to ignore the fault lines in the tension between the led and their leaders. How many of the shortcomings that are regularly alluded to in our discourse on the national condition are the result of a failure on the part of the "people" to hold their "leaders" to account? Even when we take as given the fact that the absence of institutional mechanisms for the exercise of democratic control makes it difficult, if not impossible, to demand (let alone, enforce) accountability over our political representatives, we still fail to respond adequately to the question of whose duty it is to see to it that these mechanisms are put in place and working properly.

This stream of consciousness led inevitably down the path to one question: "Was there anything in my knowledge of and association with 'Rotimi' that guaranteed he was going to make a good fist of the challenges he would have to address were he to be elected the executive governor of Rivers State?"

Difficult though it was to proffer a single word answer to this poser, it was easier to look to his pedigree as reflected above. As Speaker of the Rivers State House of Assembly from 1999 until 2007, he navigated his two terms as head of that august body with a maturity that belied both his age and experience. We have subsequently seen how these theatres of training have enabled him to design unique responses to the developmental challenges before Rivers State.

And yet, about Rotimi Amaechi there is a lot more. If you are searching for a key to unlocking this enigma, look no further than his idealistic days as an undergraduate. The time we spent together then, the intense arguments we joined in, and the concepts over which we agreed to differ as we mulled appropriate responses to the seminal issues of those times, had a special resonance as part of a perpetually questing academic community. But they have had a wider reach. For the most part, reflecting on these conversations was like looking through a peephole at the souls of my interlocutors, "psychologising" them, and putting together character profiles on their bases. In search of assurances that my friend was indeed of the right cut to lead the state, they were decidedly invaluable.

Called upon to write this foreword, my reminiscences are of a story of perseverance in the face of rather frightening odds. I was persuaded of his leadership abilities. Still, even now, I'm uncertain as to which of Rotimi Amaechi's traits I consider his strongest. His doggedness? His belief in the power of the people? His unflinching commitment to friendship? Or his strong family values? Doubtless, it was to this calibre of man that Thomas Babbington Macaulay addressed his poem "Horatius":

And how can man die better
Than facing fearful odds
For the ashes of his fathers
And the temples of his gods?

The obvious challenge implied in these lines is daunting and not easily for the faint-hearted. However, it is clear that within the governance challenge, as described by Professor Ihonvbere, there is ample space for character issues to play a catalytic role in the development process. What is the typology of these character issues? Nimi Wariboko ("Excellence as a Moral Vision for Political Leadership") contends "that the paramount community virtue is not just concerned with community well-being. The concern for the community's well-being is simultaneously a concern for what the individual person *can do* and *be* if such a person is not limited".

This, I guess, is the story of Governor Rotimi Amaechi. This collection of essays therefore provides foreground to the nature of the leadership challenge faced by our people for the many achievements of the current administration in Rivers State.

Dr. Alex Otti
Lagos, Nigeria.
October 2010

Chapter One
THE LEADERSHIP MAZE
Eme N. Ekekwe

Very often we get so obsessed with NOW, not caring for 'Nigeria two hundred years hence' even though one admits that NOW has to be properly secured in order to plan for tomorrow. But when the expediency of now predominates our undertakings, we suddenly arrive at a tomorrow we did not plan for (Jason,1998: 26; original emphasis.)

As Nigeria marked its fiftieth year of independence from Britain, one refrain could be heard from the citizens: the country's leadership, whether civilian or military, has been a disappointment. The high hopes that were evident at the time of independence have turned into ashes in the mouths of those who were glad to see the back of the British. The indices of apparent failure are all so obvious that it seems difficult for one to identify any areas of success that a majority of Nigerians would agree with – save, perhaps, the precarious survival of the country after a most hateful civil war.

There is little doubt that the performance of Nigeria's leaders has been lack-lustre, to put it mildly. There seems little doubt too that the ordinary citizen has been complicit in the evolution and survival of bad leadership in the country. There is deep meaning in the saying that a people gets the leadership it deserves; it is in part a reflection of the law of homogeneity. We will keep getting bad leaders so long as anybody can foist himself on us and literally commit murder while we shrug our shoulders without bothering to hold him accountable.

In playing what late Chief Bola Ige called "sidon look", we do not make even a small space for improved leadership to germinate and grow. Except for a precious few – like Wole Soyinka, Gani Fahwemini, Ken Saro-Wiwa, Chinua Achebe, Claude Ake, and Ebitu Ukiwe, among others - who refuse to be led by the nose, most Nigerians have hailed those who impose themselves on the country and occupied leadership positions. Of course among those who have occupied such leadership positions in the country, there have been a precious few who, if only for a moment, renewed the hope of the citizens in the possibility of taking the country to somewhere better than where they met it.

In this regard, who can easily forget Murtala Mohammed, the smartly attired general with a serious visage who led Nigeria for a few momentous months? He gave Nigerians a sense of direction and returned patriotism to governance. Mohammed showed Nigerians what they could do and where they could be with their human and material resources. In return, and even though he has been long gone from the scene, the people have remained loyal to his memory. It is doubtful that any other Nigerian leader has enjoyed such enduring loyalty.

Some may include Muhammadu Buhari and M.K.O. Abiola in the category of leaders who showed some potential to transform Nigeria. Both cases are indeed intriguing. Buhari's sense of discipline came like a breath of fresh air in the putrid world created by the then ruling National Party of Nigeria (NPN). Unfortunately, Buhari could not read the political weather well enough, and he met the warm welcome he received with a clenched iron fist. He therefore failed very early in his mission. One of the tests of leadership is the ability to persuade people to follow you freely and not make their world in your own image, no matter how well you mean for them. There is no doubting Buhari's personal credentials and patriotism, but the missteps he took in 1984 have not ceased to haunt his political career. In fact, it would appear that some vested interests would not want Nigerians to easily forget Buhari's apparent discipline, which they interpret as harshness – as if either discipline or harshness were terrible medicine in a country which its leaders have built on a foundation of "anything goes" (cf. Obasanjo, 1999). In a large measure, Buhari has shown unrealized potential as far as national leadership is concerned.

Like Buhari's, the Abiola phenomenon was more one of potential than anything else. He may have been a successful businessman, but in political leadership he offered no more than hope. But his advent in politics, we would argue, was important for a totally different reason. It would appear that his election represented a moment when the ordinary people of this country showed that if given a fairly transparent electoral process, they could rally to a cause without giving undue weight to their primordial differences. Ordinary Nigerians showed in the 1993 presidential election that they were not as divided by religion and ethnicity as some analysts would lead one to believe. In other words, the Abiola phenomenon was not about leadership as such but rather about the potential for change in the citizens.

It is instructive that the leadership fought back against the people by annulling Abiola's election. Unfortunately, the pushback in the form of various June 12 movements did not quite re-establish the power of the people. Thanks to the then president, General Ibrahim B. Babangida and his military comrades, Nigeria could not rise from the ashes.

It would be hypothetical to wonder whether Abiola's accession to power would have lifted Nigeria onto a new and higher pedestal. Those who acquired power after 1999 through so-called elections have been so remarkable in the way they exercise power without responsibility that they give a bad name to politics and democracy. Like Abiola, they were the products of the dark days of military rule. From the executive branch at federal and state levels to the legislative branch, it would appear that most of those who occupy public office are bent on dragging the nation back to the dark ages. Their personal success, so very evident in their wealth, has been built on the misery of those they were (s) elected to lead. The so-called dividends of democracy they trumpet while in office evaporate as soon as they leave that office. But they persist in office because Nigerians appear to have a great capacity for tolerating their oppressors. Jason's remark about this still resonates today: "The 'leaders' we have had so far were simply tolerated, and whatever support they got did not spring from unyielding patriotism, but from the simple fact that any change, just any change, is preferred to any existing bad 'leadership'." (Jason, 1998: 27)

An argument can be made to the effect that Nigerians are protesting rather too long and too loudly about their condition. After all, it might be said, we have only been a country for fifty years, which is very short in historical terms. According to such an argument, it would be unrealistic to expect us to be as democratic or powerful as the United States, which has been around for over 200 years. The only thing wrong with this argument is its implicit presumption that we have to go through the same stages as did America or any of the other countries we could hold up as examples of reasonable progress.

While one can concede that surely there are examples of progress that we can point to as nation, we must also admit that given the level of technology now available to mankind, and given the level of resources available to this country – oil reserves in excess of 34 billion barrels as well as gas reserves of about 155 trillion cubic feet (tcf) – we could surely have done much better if we had had the right leadership and the vision. But the question might still be asked: what leadership and what vision? That is where this book comes in.

This book was conceived as a small contribution to the definition and search for credible and responsible leadership in Nigeria. The idea was to offer some analysis of what has passed for leadership in Nigeria and from there to suggest, implicitly or explicitly, what might be required. We did not set out to produce a primer on leadership but to hold up both to our present so-called leaders and to our citizens a mirror and a compass. This is our way of contributing to the issues in the debate about improved governance and Nigeria's leadership in a way that should hold the attention of the expert and the non-expert. In doing so, we hope to encourage the emergence of the kind of leadership that could, in the long run, transform Nigeria.

Each of the contributors tried to answer the question of what leadership is in a way that is both refreshing and original. Some common elements are evident in the various views. For instance, all contributors agree that if we insist on referring to the current crop of rulers of Nigeria as leaders, we would be donning them with a toga too dignified for what they have represented so far. This is because a leader in the proper sense, according to the contributors, must have a vision of where he or she wants to take the society.

He is marked out, whether in the workplace, in a particular institution, or at any level of the society, by his quest to genuinely help his fellow citizens develop their capabilities as they try to achieve excellence. The leader must provide the roadmap for motivating individuals and the society as a whole to reach beyond themselves and achieve a future that in turn challenges them to strive for higher levels of progress.

It may seem ironic, but what emerges from these ideas is that the leader must be a servant, serving his followers with his skill and with available resources so that they improve on their achievements. It goes without saying that such a leader must be selfless and that his primary concern must be the well-being of the people. Politics for the leader is only a platform for service (which it has not been so far in Nigeria) and not a means for gaining access to the state in order to enrich oneself and one's cohorts (which is what the so-called Nigerian leader has turned it into).

That those who pass for leaders in Nigeria have largely been a disappointment is reflected in the decay in society that confronts every citizen, stifles individual initiative, and greatly dampens the spirit of patriotism. Were the right leadership in place, Nigeria, after fifty years of independence, would not be the political equivalent of a child afflicted with *kwashiorkor.* Certainly, every human and material ingredient for building a great nation is there, but the critical and necessary catalyst for doing so – good leadership – has been virtually non-existent.

Few countries in the world boast so vast a combination of gas and oil reserves, as well as a population of over 140 million people within a territory that cannot be described as hostile. This endowment notwithstanding, as Ihonvbere's contribution graphically shows, we appear to have surpassed ourselves in underachievement. It has become a commonplace to tell ourselves how Malaysians came to Nigeria and borrowed the oil palm tree, but now this nation imports Malaysian palm oil. So corrupt, so greedy, so inept and directionless has the so-called leadership of Nigeria been that it is easy to see why there has been some concern about the health of their minds (Maduka, 2010: 43–4).

In his contribution, Ekekwe attempts to trace what we might call the development of the underdevelopment of the Nigerian leadership. In part, these leaders reflect only too well the nature of the social classes from which they are recruited. Every country's leadership must have its roots in the economy of that country, the better to allow them steer its affairs in ways that protect and project its interests. In the case of Nigeria it would appear that those who occupy leadership positions have no stake in the economy and are rather ill-prepared for the role they play. Their failures put the country at risk, because they do not have any stake in its economy; they do not even put the money they make as their dividends of democracy to work in the local economy. Being largely compradors and contractors they see governance not in terms of managing the society to reach beyond itself; they see it as the awarding of contracts and the commissioning of projects that sooner or later collapse.

A most interesting perspective on what leadership is and how it should work is provided in the contribution by Wariboko. He argues for a point of view that sees leadership as the ability to engineer in people and the society a frame of mind that seeks to surpass the "now" (whatever it may be) in pursuit of fresh horizons of existence. Leadership is the ability to open the spaces in which individuals in society are able to fill in the humanity (values and potentials) within them, so that they are not seen and do not feel themselves to be just a "thing", but proper human beings, with all the rights and responsibilities from nature that pertain thereto. If one tried to analyse Nigeria's situation from the perspective provided by Wariboko, it would be obvious that we have been labouring under the wrong concepts. In our view, the interesting element in this perspective is not that it leads us to a different conclusion about Nigeria (or any other country for that matter), but that it helps us to better understand how we got where we are.

In his own contribution, Ejobowah looks at the issue of resource ownership that has been at the root of our national debate in the last two decades at least. When the military government under Lt. Col. (as he then was) Yakubu Gowon vested ownership of the mineral resources of the country in the federal government of Nigeria, it may have done so in apparent response to the exigencies of the civil war which was then raging in its bloody ferocity. The fine theoretical issues raised in Ejobowah's contribution may have had nothing to do with what the government was doing at that time. But time and circumstances have changed, and fresh questions (which call for different perspectives) are being asked with an intensity that is definitely new in the culture of public discourse in Nigeria. Ejobowah's is a thought-provoking piece that, one suspects, will excite more discussion, not just in the Niger Delta but across the country.

Our final chapter is more or less a case study to answer the question of how a leadership that once raised hopes in the community about the possibility of rising above the ordinary, ended up as another bad example. The case of the Ogoni which Nna examines is like a metaphor for the whole country. Emerging from colonialism in 1960, Nigerians expected their leaders to help build a better and enduring tomorrow. They fervently hoped that the night of dehumanization and underdevelopment that they suffered under colonialism would gradually yield to the day of glory when each citizen would be proudly Nigerian. But alas, for lack of better leadership, the so-called average Nigerian citizen who experienced colonial rule cannot say unequivocally that he is now better off. This is why it is not at all unusual to hear some Nigerians wish for a return to the colonial days. There could not be a worse condemnation of the country's leadership than is implicit in this wish, however misguided we may think those who hold it.

There is of course no reason to suggest that Nigeria's leadership cannot change and meet the challenges that confront the nation. In fact, the idea of this contribution to the leadership debate is the belief that if nothing else will, the contradictions of the present will force that change for the better. In other words, the dire circumstances they have created will force the leadership to examine its *modus operandi,* because its own members will be affected by the growing negative trends. For a very long time, Nigerian leaders largely ignored the cry for justice in the Niger Delta. When eventually it dawned on them that unless something was done, the hen that lays the proverbial golden egg might die, and they might have no nation to rule, it concentrated their minds, at least for a while. How far this will go is anybody's guess, but at least for a while there is a window of opportunity for possible radical review and change.

The contributors to this book have no illusion that tomorrow morning Nigeria will get a crop of leadership that inspires hope because it has the vision, the discipline, and a roadmap for achieving that vision. But we do believe that we ought to contribute by encouraging and nurturing even the weakest signs of change for the better. This is because contemplating the perpetuation of the *status quo* is rather depressing. The prospects of revolutionary change that will usher in the kind of leadership we would wish for are rather remote. We must therefore live with the philosophy of gradualism. As Wariboko has argued here, it would appear that any development that can be properly so called is achieved through optimizing and consolidating the possibilities of the moment. What is important is to ensure that the present is consciously transformed into the future, with due cognizance taken of the past.

Of course we have seen leaders in this country who seemed to have the capacity for charting a new course but who later disappointed such expectations. However, the possibility that someone who starts off showing encouraging signs of good leadership could still slide back to retrogression should not deter us from applauding and encouraging those positive traits that are now evident. It could give those who show such encouraging signs fresh wind to push on; it might inspire others to see that any little good they can do would help. Let each person or each party do what they must and leave the rest to history.

In taking our stand of trying in our little way to encourage the emergence of good leadership, we have obviously been political. Indeed, anybody who takes a position on any public issue is by definition political, so this is not strange. But what we certainly are not, in any objective sense, is partisan. Partisanship in matters of this kind would degrade what could otherwise be noble ideas. We only intend the following chapters as a vital contribution to a critical debate. That is the strength of this book.

We have painted with a wide brush and in bold colours the problem with leadership in Nigeria. This in itself is something that many Nigerians know or feel, even though they do not clothe their knowledge and feelings about it with the same theoretical or academic flourish we have demonstrated here. But we have tried to go beyond this by promoting the underlying *nuances* that are already beginning to stir in the system – nuances that we hope will become bolder as the political space eventually becomes less poisonous. All the chapters point to these nuances.

This book is eventually about hope, not dreadful disappointments; positive potentials, not crushing certainties.

It would not matter how long we stand and wring our hands in pain and regret. What is important is that we gird our loins to work in whatever field we choose and encourage those nuances we sense in the present that might yield a better tomorrow for the Nigerian nation. There may be no evident seismic cracks in the political and economic terrain, but we can put our foot into the small openings and hope to widen them so that fresh air brings life to the seed of promise.

Chapter Two
THE NIGERIAN LEADERSHIP QUESTION
Eme N. Ekekwe

Introduction:

One of the few things we know for certain about Nigeria, besides its being so richly endowed that it has great potential, is that it has serious leadership problems. It is difficult to disagree with Chinua Achebe that Nigeria has not achieved anything near the potential made possible by its endowments because of poor leadership. Just how deep an insight Achebe has on the Nigerian leadership situation can easily be gleaned from some of his fictional and non-fictional writing. Anybody who has read his *A Man of the People* with a political eye cannot fail to see how accurately he portrays, in lurid and comical pictures, the tragedy that is the failure of the Nigerian political leadership. In his 1983 work, *The Trouble with Nigeria*, he pulls no punches in declaring that if Nigeria had credible leadership, the country would not be the incapacitated elephant it has become.

More than two decades since Achebe diagnosed the trouble with Nigeria, the situation has only worsened. The country continues to rely for its economic and political survival mainly on crude oil, and to produce and export this product, it is largely dependent on foreign technology and know-how!

The minimum that any state worthy of the name owes its citizens is security of life and property. But insecurity threatens to overwhelm the Nigerian citizen, while the state does not appear to have any comprehensive strategy for dealing with it. This is a nation where even members of the ruling class, let alone ordinary citizens, are bumped off and the police fail to uncover the perpetrators: recall Dele Giwa, Chief Alfred Rewane, Chief Bola Ige, Chief Harry Marshall, to name some of the most prominent.

Further, more than two decades after the Ibrahim Badamasi Babangida regime made a song and dance about diversifying the economy, Nigeria continues to be a one-product economy that cannot use even this one product to light up its darkness. It is disturbing that a country like Nigeria repeatedly fails to enforce human rights, to conduct a fair and violence-free election, or to provide and maintain basic physical and human infrastructure. Billions of dollars in revenue in successive years have not been deployed to reduce the poverty, unemployment, and poor nutrition that ravage both the urban and rural populations. Social services have practically collapsed, and the managers of the state have constituted themselves into a burden on the system. The space for the development of individual initiative has been choked up by corruption and bureaucratic red tape. Anybody trying to get a post office box in present-day Nigeria (when even letter writing is going out of style) will come up against a swath of papers that can only discourage the effort. A recent study shows that registering businesses in Nigeria – a process which should have been made very easy in order to encourage investment - takes a much longer time than is necessary (World Bank, 2010).

How do we explain this uncomplimentary background? We readily agree with Achebe that the trouble with Nigeria is bad leadership. But we need to go a step further here and try to understand why that leadership has been bad and why for the foreseeable future it might remain so. This is not to write off Nigeria as a nation. On the contrary, it is done to enable us see the depth of the problem so that it can be better managed and solved.

We shall discuss the issue in three main parts. In the first part, we try to clarify the concept of leadership. In the second part, we apply the important elements of that concept and see how so-called leadership in Nigeria measures up and thereby try to locate the trouble, if any, with it. In the third part, we look at what might be done to "move the nation forward" – to borrow a favourite cliché of Nigeria's political rulers.

What Is Leadership?

All over the world there is a leadership deficit. Precious few are they who have any vision, no matter how faint, of how to lead the world out of its protracted problems. The clearest manifestation of this is in the disenchantment which citizens in many countries feel with their political and economic managers, the ruling class. For sure, neither Nigeria in particular nor the world in general has lacked for prominent men and women in all fields of endeavour who would be flattered to be described as leaders. But that they are mostly impostors to that dignified title is evident in the parlous situation that exists in Nigeria or in many issues on a worldwide scale, such as in the fight against hunger and poverty or in dealing with the Middle East crisis.

It is interesting to note that this global leadership deficit appears to be at its highest just when the world has been inundated with concepts and theories of leadership and management. We have seen in the recent past how so-called management gurus have saturated the field of corporate management studies with various theories of leadership. But no sooner was the ink dry on these theories than the explosion of a series of corporate crises hit the major centres of capital in the late 1900s and early 2000s. Among other things, the crisis in the American company Enron, for example, showed just how hollow were the theories of leadership that were being marketed. It is our view that all this is the result of lack of clarity of the concept.

Without getting into the existing theories about leadership, we would argue that it is important to separate leadership from rulership, even though the leader could also be a ruler. For us, leadership is, in part, about working with others and making tangible and measurable impact in specific areas and over a specific period. The scale of the impact is not important: it could be in the family, at school, in a community, or at national or international levels. What is critical is that the acknowledged leader takes his team from wherever they may be to a recognizable and (preferably) better place. Leadership is not just about occupying the position of the leader. It is not just about mobilizing men and material to achieve a defined end - which really is management - even though the leader must do just that or get others to do it on his behalf and at his behest. But he or she must do more. For us leadership is the unique ability of an individual or a group of individuals to "see a positive world that lies beyond tomorrow", so to speak; to excite others in the possibility of achieving what is seen; and to have (most of) them willingly participate or cooperate in ensuring its achievement or completion with available resources. That which lies beyond tomorrow may be expressed as, for lack of a better word, a "project", where project is not something physical such as a road or an electrical installation that merely calls for awarding contracts.

As is implied in the foregoing, a leadership project must involve a vision, which vision provides the context and goal for activities within the polity or organization. The vision is the necessary "software", and the goals (the activities that people engage in) and specific milestones for its achievement are the "hardware". There can be no question of leadership unless there is a vision which drives efforts under it. The vision must excite the possibility of something better than what exists – something inspiring and positively larger than the contemporary. Achieving the vision of a leadership could be done in two mutually reinforcing ways: in a positive way by building or strengthening channels of moral and lawful conduct, and in a negative way by removing obstacles that militate against the fullest achievement of individual initiative and potential.

Here we would emphasize and expatiate on two things. First is that the project undertaken by the leadership must lead to some observable improvement in the lives of members of the community or of humanity in general. The project must be "enduring", meaning that more than one generation of the beneficiaries would be positively touched by its impact. Second, we would emphasize that the potential beneficiaries, having been persuaded about the positive impact of the project, must be seen to "willingly participate or cooperate" in its achievement. We would argue that any element of compulsion or coercion is virtually alien to the concept of leadership. This is not to say that there may not be instances when the leadership will have to compel a section of the people to do the manifestly needful in the general interest. It is to say, however, that as a rule, coercion and leadership cannot go together.

If it is meaningful, leadership must bring about some degree of development of or movement to better values, standards, and expectations. Note that not just any kind of development or movement is involved. There could be two types of movement or development. One is forward and positive, and is, therefore, progress. The other type is backward and negative; such a movement or development would actually be retrogression. Needless to say, few rational beings would see the latter as desirable. But we must further distinguish this from stagnation which could occur even when there is movement. The analogy of the rocking chair is very apt here. The question as to what constitutes progress could be open to wide debate because it cannot be presumed to be always obvious and objective. No doubt an element of subjectivity is involved: the followers have both the right and the responsibility to decide whether what is proposed is, for them, progress or not. This presumes that they would have an opportunity to exercise their free will in this regard.

Now, it is important to further stress that leadership must be distinguished from a related phenomenon – demagoguery. Demagoguery presents similar qualities as leadership; both claim to lead to higher goals. But the latter is real and the former is decidedly false. We may say, on account of the apparent similarities between them but in recognition of their fundamental differences, that demagoguery is a malformation or degeneration of leadership. Leadership is objective and has a large purpose – the interest of a majority of the followers. On the other hand, demagoguery is self-serving and has only a limited purpose – the interest of the demagogue and his clique. Where demagoguery further degenerates, it becomes clear dictatorship. Thus, one must keenly distinguish between leadership, demagoguery, and dictatorship. This is not easy because they present what appear to be similar features, but whereas leadership awakens spontaneous and positive reaction from the public, demagoguery has to coax similar reaction from them through some kind of persuasion. When demagoguery degenerates into dictatorship, it must rely on coercion and brute force.

Both demagoguery and dictatorship make ample use of propaganda.

The demagogue or dictator may be able to drive a population to achieve some major physical project, but (as so often happens) no sooner does he fall than many of his projects are consigned to the dustbin of history. These projects do not last in the hearts and minds of the same people from whom sweat and tears were coerced in order to make the achievements. Consider in this regard the fate of the major projects undertaken by the likes of Adolf Hitler in Germany, Benito Mussolini in Italy, Pol Pot in Cambodia, Idi Amin in Uganda, and Sanni Abacha in Nigeria, to name the worst and most obvious in the pack.

Leadership is not the same as rulership, although both imply the exercise of authority. Dictators and demagogues may be rulers because they impose their will on the society instead of allowing for the free flow of currents of free will. They "rule in" what they want and "rule out" what they do not want. Whereas the leader depends on the followers' voluntarily participation to achieve the vision, the demagogue and the dictator have to force compliance. The voluntary disposition that characterizes leadership is rooted in the fact that those in the community see and share the vision of the leader; they see in the vision or organization values which accord with their own. This is not necessarily so under the demagogue or dictator. The will of the followers is not given free rein here, and so only coercion can produce or secure the necessary compliance.

Leadership must be further distinguished from personal initiative or resourcefulness, even though the leader must have initiative and be quite resourceful. This is because initiative or resourcefulness can be the preserve of the manager who is not necessarily a leader, and it can be as potent in a private context as in a social one. Leadership involves working with others who may be followers or managers. Initiative or resourcefulness does not necessarily require this social context to manifest itself. A man marooned on an uninhabited island needs initiative and resourcefulness to return to civilization, but he is not thereby displaying leadership. In a similar vein, we would go further and say on this ground that Machiavelli's notes in *The Prince* have less to do with leadership and statesmanship than with political tactics in the use of power by a ruler. The Prince has only a personal ambition – to acquire and retain power. There is no higher purpose here since those who are under the Prince's rule are either more or less passive or are coerced by the Prince's brutality.

It should not surprise us that some social situations tend to produce or facilitate the emergence of a specific set of leaders. There may indeed be a "man for all seasons", but it is very rare, if at all possible, to have a leader for all occasions and situations who is human. Thus it is important to understand leaders within the social context of their emergence and operation. Take Nigeria in the mid-1960s, for instance. The January 1966 coup threw up a situation in which the Yakubu Gowons and the Odumegwu Ojukwus emerged as so-called leaders. So long as the situation persisted that defined the *raison d'etre* of their leadership (in Gowon's case to reunite Nigeria, and in Ojukwu's case to give Igbos the security which Nigeria had denied them), they remained leaders because they had a vision that resonated with the people. Remove or change the situation that produced such people, and they disappear from the leadership position and may even become just as ordinary as the next man or woman. If they insist on occupying the leadership position they automatically transform into rulers. Who would have thought that the once-popular Gowon would, quoting Shakespeare as he did so, leave from the scene unceremoniously, on his way to becoming a fugitive in Britain a few short years later, or that Ojukwu, the very man on whose every word most people in the breakaway Republic of Biafra hung during the civil war, would have woefully lost an election in the 1980s among the very people he had led?

This should say something to us about the ephemeral nature of rulership, just like the power with which it cloaks itself – quite unlike leadership that leaves a sweet taste in the mouth long after the leader is gone. Who would easily forget a Nelson Mandela? The elusiveness of rulership should alert us to the fact that it is possible for one individual to cross the line from leadership into demagoguery, or from the latter into dictatorship. Very often an individual may start off appearing as a genuine leader, but over time he gets imperceptibly corrupted and begins to see himself as indispensable. Or, because he came into office with a vision that held mass appeal, he begins to see himself as the messiah.

Such was the case of many African leaders in the nationalist and immediate post-colonial periods. In West Africa, there was Kwame Nkrumah, whose theories about imperialism, African unity, liberation, and the dignity of the black man held appeal across the continent but who later saw himself as the "osagyefo" or saviour and president-for-life in Ghana. A parallel case in East Africa is that of Robert G. Mugabe of Zimbabwe. It was easy to see the points at which Nkrumah or Mugabe crossed the line as they more and more relied on repression to hang onto office. Both cases are to be further distinguished from those of impostors like Jean Boukassa in Central Africa, who cannot be accused of having ever tried to be leaders in the sense we argue here.

Another point already alluded to above but worthy of some emphasis is that leadership is to be found in many levels and sectors of society and in different fields of human endeavour, not just at the apex. Those who occupy positions at the different levels must act in concert with those at the apex to produce coherent leadership. Leadership may be likened to a pyramid: below that apex there is a supporting corps of persons who play leadership roles as union leaders, student movement leaders, professional association leaders, youth leaders, the clergy, leaders of women's organizations, etc. These may be leaders in their own right, and failure or success at their level invariably reflects on the national or wider situation sooner or later. Sometimes their views may even be opposed to those of the occupants of the apex, but the point is that the interplay between them and those at the apex is what gives the full flavour of the overall leadership in a society.

We believe it is a misconception of leadership to focus only on those who happen to occupy positions at the political apex. It is understandable that they tend to attract more notice because of the breadth of the political space over which they appear to play and because they can set the tone of the overall leadership direction. But this does not necessarily make them any better by definition than leaders at other levels. At best, and only because of the constituency he has, this would make the leader a sort of *primus inter pares*. However, unless the leaders' visions, programmes, and policies are duly synchronized with those at the lower, less visible levels, the society will suffer bad leadership. If our position is correct, then studies of leadership that focus on the apex would be seriously flawed, and the real challenge of such studies is to show how the different levels synchronize to achieve designated goals.

One does not have to be an expert in the field to see that even scholars have been rather commonsensical in the way they categorize leaders: party leaders, business leaders, academic leaders, or opinion leaders. There is a certain lack of rigor in the way the concept has been understood.

Of those who have helped to clarify this issue, it seems to us that Plato made the most serious effort to examine the nature and structure of leadership from a perspective beyond the ordinary. First, he recognized the need to locate leadership in a social context: the philosopher-king emerged from the group of guardians and represented the elite within this group. Second, Plato recognized that the leader must have clarity about where he wants to take the society: the philosopher-king gained such clarity through his search for the uncommon meaning of reality, thus demonstrating that leadership is not an all-comers affair. No matter the level at which he is involved, the leader must be prepared for the role he is to assume. It calls for dedication and sacrifice, which not everybody can make. Third, the leader works for the general interest because only in serving that interest does he fulfil his leadership mission. Fourth, the leader must be humble. Were the philosopher-king conceited and arrogant, he would not have hesitated to jump into the leadership position, waving his superior knowledge. Fifth, the followers (other groups in the city-state) willingly submitted to the leader, recognizing that they would be fulfilled only in the context and content of that leadership. In return, these other groups in *The Republic* worked to provide the security and material needs of the philosopher-king, while he, in a situation of equal exchange, served their moral and spiritual needs. Here was a balanced reciprocal exchange in which rulers and the ruled benefited from each other's mutual support. The basis for such leadership was service for mutual growth. If we apply these attributes to what passes for leadership in Nigeria, it will be fairly easy to see why things are in such a sad state in our land.

From the above, we can say that leadership is a sacred duty which places on the one involved the responsibility of helping many others realize their potential as human beings as he himself realizes his own potential in that context.

It is an opportunity to serve and, in serving, to develop potentials that lie dormant in the "servant". Between the leader and his followers there must be a balance in the flows of service and loyalty. Where service is not given by the leader, he cannot have loyalty. He might have followers who submit – they may even be cowed (ask the late General Abacha) - for a while, but they will eventually revolt because submission is patently unnatural as far as human beings are concerned. Circumstances may oblige the individual to appear to submit, but sooner or later he will rise, overtly or subtly, in rebellion.

The Troubled Foundation of Nigerian Leadership:

From the foregoing analysis, it seems that Nigeria has hardly any leaders in the sense we are arguing. The closest we came was in the first generation of people who led the nationalist struggle. They had a high ideal or vision: to liberate the country from colonialism, which denied the basic humanity of the colonized (Ekekwe, 1998). They helped the people in general regain confidence in themselves and in their innate abilities, and they offered the citizens (some would say unrealistic) hope of a better future. It is noteworthy that the anti-colonial struggles still resonate even with those who were born after that era. But the success of the struggle also produced its own contradictions, as the leaders began to buckle under the pressure of ethnicity and the politics of scarcity. In the immediate post-independence years, leadership began to degenerate into demagoguery and to tend towards dictatorship. This lowest stage was reached with the arrival at Government House of military boots and starched uniforms following the January 1966 *coup d'etat*.

To understand the quality and character of so-called leadership in Nigeria, it is important to appreciate its class character. In pre-independence Nigeria, leadership was drawn from the petty bourgeoisie. Increasingly, through various means that do not concern us here, this class yielded the largely commercial bourgeois class as the main source of leadership recruitment, especially at the higher echelons. Whereas in the nationalist and immediate post-independence era the leadership was drawn from the civil professions (school teachers, journalists, medical practitioners, and public servants), increasingly they are coming from business people, contractors, and other appendages to those who have had access to the state apparatus (retired senior civil servants, many of whom served under the military, and former senior military officers or their protégés). In the era when the petty bourgeoisie provided the source of leadership, money was not a major reason for going into politics.

But not any more: for those who want to get into the so-called leadership ranks at all levels, money is a critical factor. This is what manifests itself as the now-prevalent phenomenon of "godfatherism", which was hitherto absent in Nigeria's political lexicon. Of course, many past leaders were invited into the political arena by those already established there – the Nnamdi Azikiwes, the Ahmadu Bellos, and the Obafemi Awolowos. But Azikiwe, Bello, and Awolowo were acknowledged by these people as their mentors, not as their godfathers in the sense made notorious by Dr Chris Ngige and Chief Chris Uba in the politics of Anambra State. The difference is that in recent times, politics has degenerated from being a call to public service and has become a mere business deal, as supposed leadership, which used politics as its vehicle, also degenerated into demagoguery.

Owing to the historical circumstances of its evolution, the first generation of Nigerian leaders may be said to have been ill-prepared or inexperienced for the roles they were to be trusted with. This inexperience was apparent in the low level of education that most of those who were in political leadership at various levels had. Compare this to the lengthy political training and tutelage their counterparts in other parts of the world undergo. Mostly teachers and journalists, those who lit and carried the torch of nationalism and nation-building had only limited acquaintance with the sort of exposure and experience needed to fashion a nation-state out of the more than 350 ethnic nationalities that comprise Nigeria. It is understandable, therefore, that they took the path of least resistance and often retreated into their ethnic laager at the first signs of opposition, as did Awolowo, Zik, and Bello.

Nor has this lack of preparation for a leadership role in a complex society changed. Consider that the soldiers who shot their way to power after January 1966 found that they were swimming in infested waters. For all his idealism, Major Chukwuma Nzeogwu appeared to be lost in the national role he took up. Major-General Aguiyi- Ironsi did not fare any better. It is instructive in this regard that General Yakubu Gowon went to school to read Political Science *after* nearly a decade at the apex of Nigeria's political structure. General Olusegun Obasanjo too went to get some university education after two terms as Nigeria's head of state. We could multiply the example at various levels.

The ruling class from which the national leadership has emerged has been apparently interested in only one thing: private personal accumulation. This has been traced by various scholars (e.g. Ekekewe, 1986; Ake, 1996; Ihnovbere, 1994) to the nature of the colonial economy and politics that threw up this class. Excluded from meaningful participation in the colonial economy, the petty bourgeois elements that rose to political leadership quickly began to use the post-colonial state for personal enrichment. This imbued the struggle for access or (what is the same thing) for a place on the leadership ladder with the life-and-death tone it still has today. Many Nigerians, especially the political class, screamed foul when former President Obasanjo described the 2007 elections as a "do or die affair". Those who did so were only being hypocritical, for Obasanjo voiced an incontrovertible and obvious fact. Most of the politicians who took exception to that fact very likely went on to be part of the massive rigging machine that was deployed in the course of those same elections.

It is evident that this disposition to accumulate has grown over the decades to envelope other classes whose members may be recruited into any public office. The most obvious form in which it manifests itself is corruption, which has become endemic in the entire economy. It used to be limited only to those who occupied positions in the state apparatus and to members of the dominant class. No more. To the many Nigerians who fight for leadership or management positions in the public and private sectors at every level, occupying such positions is not the means to public service and to building up the nation. Rather it has become the trough from which they must drink to their hearts' content. There are of course exceptions, but they are the exceptions that confirm the rule. So obsessed are the political and economic elites with the drive for personal accumulation that they have even lost sight of their own class' interest, to the extent that this class now threatens itself and the nation. But space does not allow us to discuss these issues here.

Recruited mainly from a class that comprises contractors and commercial interests, the so-called Nigerian leadership sees its role in "cash and carry" terms. Consider, as Onomo (2010) reports, that "out of the 2009 annual budget of N3.1 trillion, N1.3 trillion or 42% ended up as remuneration for 17,500 individuals [who occupy positions within the state apparatus] in a country of 150 million people." And this sum is their "legitimate" entitlement. These are members of a class that has no patience to nurture anything (since they can sign away such huge sums without sweat) or pursue excellence, nor has it any apparent commitment to a vision of the Nigerian economy in which its interests are best protected.

In fact, the idea of building or forming anything is strange to this leadership class. Building and forming require hard work, something to which this class appears allergic. We need only look at the economy to see that this class is virtually absent in industry; what space it occupies is largely in finance, contracting, and commerce. This is why, for instance, the nation would rather import refined fuel and export crude oil instead of engaging in local refining activities. Every economic activity that involves sustained hard work, discipline, and husbanding of resources that this class and the leadership has undertaken eventually fails: steel manufacturing in Ajaokuta and Aladja; paper manufacturing in Oku Iboku; aluminum smelting in Ikot Abasi; petroleum refining in Port Harcourt, Warri, and Kaduna; and fertilizer production in Onne. And rather than generate and distribute power itself, it would sooner open up the borders to import generating sets. Each of these areas of the economy requires discipline and unrelenting hard work, against a background of a clear vision of the kind of society to be built and sustained.

In every state, the ruling class must be very clear about how it wants to achieve and sustain its class projects, and this is usually based on its stake in the economy. This is what it presents as its ideology, which ideology it then, in turn, presents as that of the entire society – in some cases using such intoxicating phrases as "we, the people". To the extent that this ideology resonates with the rest of society (because it may touch on points that, liberally translated, would seem to have included the interest of other classes), it is easy for that ruling class to mobilize resources and demand sacrifices in order to assure the achievement of the vision in the ideology.

In the case of the Nigerian ruling class, it has difficulty coming up with a coherent ideology since it has no great stake in the economy; it is satisfied to collect rent from oil exploration and commerce. If it has any challenge, it is how to share the rent amongst the different levels of the so-called leadership. It has interpreted what passes for its ideology of development so narrowly to mean private accumulation that the rest of society, which has a different interpretation, is literally now de-linked from the leadership. All the noise about the "dividends of democracy" rings hollow because there is nothing in these so-called dividends that a good military government did not do or could not have done.

This ideology of development has four sub-themes: ethnicity, anti-corruption, religion, and resource control. Even though most of the leadership at all levels in society is involved in it, none wants to admit that corruption has become a veritable element of Nigeria's economic culture and that it is fed by the desire for personal accumulation. Rather, every leader in every sector and at all levels adorns himself and his office with some anti-corruption toga. The result is that even as every leader promises to rid society of the obnoxious habit, it grows from regime to regime, military or civilian. This fits only too well into the religious and ethnicity elements. Every president, state governor, and local government chairman belongs to one religious organization or another. Even though Nigeria is supposedly a secular state, many government houses boast of chapels or mosques and in many public offices the day starts with prayers. Ironically, as these activities grow, so does corruption. The religious leaders appear only too happy to exploit the power and largesse that comes from associating with the political elites. Between these two leadership groups who should be a counterbalance to each other in the interest of the society, there is an unwritten alliance. It is noteworthy that the former head of state General Gowon leads the organization called

"Nigeria Prays". And why would it not pray? The country he once ruled is on its knees!

The very new element in the ideological mix is the theme of resource control. It was originally the brainchild of militant youths in the Niger Delta, and it was the major resolution these youths took at their congress in Kiama in 1998. It has now been hijacked by younger groups in the Nigerian leadership in the Delta as a major tool in their struggle for access to the state and for enlarging the resources for personal aggrandizement. The foul, putrid air of allegations of massive corruption that trail the likes of James Ibori, who virtually came to personify the struggle for resource control (cf. Dara), does not suggest otherwise. Under the cover of the popularity of the struggle for resource control, many rogue elements embarked on the lucrative business of illegal oil bunkering. This group is ready, under cover of the amnesty programme, to metamorphose into being legitimate players in the political arena.

Let us observe parenthetically that, interestingly, the demand for resource control, which was initially (and is still, in some pockets) resented by many elite groups outside the Niger Delta, is gaining wider significance and acceptance. This is not really because of a sudden realization of the injustice hitherto done to the Delta as a result of the prevailing national revenue sharing structure. It appears to have dawned on these other groups that resource control could – indeed has – become a veritable tool for diverting resources from the commonwealth into narrower channels for easy appropriation. Thus we have seen politicians from the some of the northern states arguing for a special commission to cater to the interests of the areas from which the nation's electricity is generated.

Of course, the political class does not present these issues in the same light that is argued here. It is trying to reformulate the ideology of development into a veritable roadmap to guide the achievement of the Nigeria project. To support this, examples could be drawn from the Vision 2010 and Vision 20-2020 projects that are supposed to mobilize Nigerians to grow the national economy to such a level that the country could join the globalized world economy as a major player. Never original in its thinking, the ruling class borrowed the vision's concept from south-east Asian countries which had used it as a vehicle to develop their economies. However, it conveniently forgot that the apparent success of the vision's model in that part of the world, was largely due to the fact that the ruling classes there were coherent and highly disciplined (even if, as in Malaysia, the coherence was of the enforced variety). Thus, in Nigeria the concept has become bastardized, and it has been difficult to get it off the ground. It is clear to any serious observer that neither under Abacha nor now under the Yar'Adua/Jonathan administration was the leadership focused on achieving such a dream. There is no index of development in either vision which is being pursued in any systematic way. Obasanjo promised that his administration would improve power generation and distribution, but eight years and billions of naira later the situation was no better than he found it. These visions have failed to achieve one of the important goals of any ideology – to link the leadership to the citizens.

If the foregoing might be regarded as the characteristics of the class from which the nation's leadership is recruited, what then are the attributes of the political elite that emerged from this class? As we will try to show, some of these characteristics of leadership derive directly from those of the entire class for, as an adage has it, the offspring of the snake is always long! In our view, those who aspire to be Nigerian leaders display characteristics that cannot in any way help to nurture the nation to higher levels of achievement and excellence. These include:

- Crass materialism, which in turn yields
- Anti-intellectualism and
- Opportunism

If we understood the interplay between these mutually reinforcing attributes, as well as how they relate to the ideology of the entire ruling class, perhaps we could begin to understand why the nation experiences acute an leadership deficit even though there is no shortage of prominent persons in leadership positions in both the private and public sector.

Crass materialism and corruption go hand in hand, and we need add little here except to observe that they in turn give rise to anti-intellectualism. The Nigerian leadership is hugely disinterested in ideas and debates. There has been hardly a Nigerian leader who welcomed debates on his policies or who saw reason to promote education beyond broad statements of support for the sector. This was worse during the military era. Then the Buhari/Idiagbon team warned against the propagation of any form of ideology. Babangida, notwithstanding the fact that he was advised by some of the country's best academics, quickly threw away the results of the debate he organised on dealings with the World Bank and later warned those opposed to his structural adjustment programme (SAP) to desist because the was no alternative to it – which really meant he was not interested in any alternative (Babagida, 1996). As for Obasanjo, it has been said (Jeyifo, 2010: 33) that he "could not brook 'correction' or refutation from anybody, and he acted from instincts not from the head or the heart, but way below the neck from the appetitive regions of the belly and the loins. And he produced and reproduced men and women like himself all over the states of the federation …" As for examples of opportunism, we can look at the frequent movements from one party to another by politicians; these need not delay us further.

Which Way Nigerian Leadership?

It is easy to see from the foregoing why it appears that Nigeria is perpetually at the cross-roads. The country's enormous potential has not been realized, regardless of the huge sums of money that have reportedly been invested in infrastructure and human development. What passes for leadership in the here has been anything but that. The country's politicians at all levels have lost respect, and even those among them who may be innocent are viewed in the popular mind as dangerous parasites on the state and on the economy of the nation.

However, there are indications that the contradictions in the system might yet yield unexpected but positive changes. It is difficult at the moment to determine the parameters or depth of the changes that may emerge, but it is safe to say that something is rumbling in the bowels of the body politic. Were the country to have serious opposition parties, it would have been easy to see the possible platform on which the changes will emerge. But with the People's Democratic Party (PDP) seemingly so well entrenched, the picture that dominates the mind is that of a band of buccaneers bent on milking the land dry. However, there are signs of hope both within and outside the ruling party. A few instances may be cited.

Take the cases of two examples from the PDP. There is the former governor of Cross River State, Donald Duke. If popular reports are anything to go by, he stood just that much above the mediocrity of the time and seemed to know what to do in office beyond awarding contracts. If in no other area, Donald Duke gave Cross River State a cultural profile that has come to stay. One may have issues with the content of this cultural profile, but the point is that is that it has helped give the people of Cross River State some identity and pride. His successor has continued to build on it. We may also cite the contribution of the late President Umaru Musa Yar'Adua who tended to be more respectful of the rulings of the judiciary even when these went against his party. Even though he had an attorney general who muddied the waters, credit must go to Yar'Adua for returning some meaning to the concept and practice of the rule of law. He also began a process that might yet help to restore dignity to the people of the Niger Delta. These initiatives were often mismanaged and only partially implemented, but in a country that has been much abused and militarized, they are not at all insignificant. Put them against the mindless invasion of Odi community in Bayelsa State under former President Obasanjo, and it becomes clear that there has been some positive movement.

There are also the likes of Governor Babatunde Fashola of Lagos State and Governor Chibuike Amaechi of Rivers State. Fashola and Amaechi seem to be trying to set a political agenda in their states that would improve how society and the economy are run, and thus give room for people to find greater fulfilment. They seem capable of looking beyond today and seeing a better future for themselves and those they lead. In doing so, they have shown uncommon courage which has, at least to some extent, set them apart from the mainstream of the elite group to which they belong.

The legacies these men are building may be open to debate, and we must recognize that theirs is but a small step, but they are no less important on this account, especially against the very dismal background from which they have arisen. It may also be argued that they (unusually) have enough resources to do what they are doing. But this should not take anything away from them; after all it is easy to have the resources and not know what to do with them or – what is the same thing – misapply the resources.

It is obvious that Nigeria needs radical changes, but one must be realistic enough to see that the progress we must have will come in fits and starts. It is possible but by no means certain that the rays of hope we see in the few examples cited here – and there may well be others – will grow and attract new players with similar tendencies into the political arena. Then Nigeria may begin getting leaders who will eventually replace the majority of rulers (demagogues and dictators) who now occupy and choke up the leadership landscape.

REFERENCES

Ake, Claude (1996). *Democracy and Development in Africa.* Washington: the Brookings Institution.

Ekekwe, Eme (1986). *Class and State in Nigeria.* London: Longman.

Ekekwe, Eme (1998). *Decolonization: The Word According to Fanon.* Port Harcourt: Amajov & Coy Nig.

Ihonvbere, Julius (1994). *Nigeria: The Politics of Adjustment and Democracy.* New Brunswick, N.J: Transaction Publishers.

Jason, Pini (1998). *A Familiar Road.* Lagos: Pinicilla Ltd.

Maduka, Chidi (2010). *Taming the Beast in the Body Politic: Culture, Nationhood, and the Imperative of Order in Nigeria.* 6th School of Graduate Studies Public Lecture Series, University of Port Harcourt.

Obasanjo, Olusegun (1993). "The Country of Anything Goes", *New York Review of Books.* Vol. 45, No. 14.

Omoruyi, Omo (1999). *The Tale of June 12*. London: Press Alliance Networks Limited.

Onomo, A. A. (2010). "Democracy: When Costs Outweigh Benefits", *The Guardian* (Lagos), Sunday, August 29

World Bank (2010). *Doing Business in Nigeria 2010*. Washington: The World Bank.

Chapter Three
LEADERSHIP AND GOOD GOVERNANCE IN NIGERIA
Julius O. Ihonvbere

The leadership question has become rather topical in Nigeria. It is now very convenient to explain away all inadequacies and blame all problems on "bad leadership". The situation is so bad that we see pockets of authoritarian nostalgia all over the country. This is the situation where people, out of frustration with the antics and repression of the custodians of state power, simply wish that the earlier repressive regimes would return! When a people wish for the pain, domination, exploitation, and abuses of the past as a reflection of the conditions in which they find themselves, it means that the structures of state power, the deployment of raw power, the patterns of accumulation, and the broad character of leadership are problematic.

While it is easy to blame all failures on leadership, and there are very valid reasons for doing so, the truth remains that leadership in itself, however defined, is a precipitate or product of socio-economic, cultural, and political arrangements in society. Consequently, leadership reflects the reality of society, the patterns of power and accumulation, and the options open to the custodians of power at any point in time. This is not to say that there are no real openings or what one may call Islands of integrity and honour, even in the most corrupt or badly led society. Rather, it simply means that it is often difficult for a thoroughly corrupted, contaminated, distorted, and disarticulated society to produce the sort of rational leaders required to bring about purposeful change. Whenever such leaders emerge, they are often harassed, domesticated, incorporated, and corrupted. The cycle of bad leadership, bad policy, and bad governance is reproduced.

In the rest of this short chapter, we investigate the relationship between good governance and leadership. It is a sort of chicken-and-egg problem: is it good governance that produces good leadership or is it the other way round? This is not to say that we are not interested in followership. In fact, it is the combination of leadership and followership that often determines the future of a nation. However, since leaders control and dominate the commanding heights of the economy, exercise legal monopoly over the means of coercion, dominate the structures and institutions of politics and economy, and shape the ideological or philosophical direction of society, we shall focus on leaders and the future.

What Is Leadership?

I will not go into a debate as to whether leaders are born or made. Suffice it to note that we are all leaders in different ways. An emergency or a challenging situation can produce leaders. For instance, an accident scene can produce a leader – someone with skills, courage, experience, and vision to take the lead, provide assistance, and mobilise others to rescue the accident victims. Even criminals like armed robbers have their own leaders, just as do churches, soccer teams, trade unions, human rights organisations, governments, and academic institutions. However, the nature of society, existing contradictions and opportunities, power balances, and societal values can determine whether the imbued leadership qualities can be nurtured, subverted, or simply negated and ignored. Leadership can be individual or collective. Either way, the purpose of leadership at home, at work, or anywhere for that matter is to exercise power, provide direction, encourage and inspire others, show the right direction, build appropriate legacies for future generations, and work for the common or public good. Leadership is therefore the capacity and ability to build a vision about the future based on a strategic, dialectical, and holistic appreciation of the past and present. It is the scale of this capacity to envision, strategize, and implement ideas and policies that produces different grades of leadership from the mediocre to the effective and efficient brands.

The Nigerian Reality in History

Nigeria's history is replete with accounts of great men and women who provided leadership at the most positive and effective levels. What is obvious is that as we move from ancient times through the colonial to the post-colonial periods, we begin to see a dilution and contamination of leadership, especially its isolation, personalisation, and divorce from the communal, cultural, and even spiritual values and regulations that shaped the emergence, nurturing, and performance of leaders. In place of exploits in war, the ability to cultivate large farmlands, the size of the yam barns, the capacity to make reasonable contributions at meetings at the village square, and other community-anchored yardsticks, the emergence of leaders shifted to the ability to engage in primitive accumulation of capital, seize power violently, form and use cabals to grab power, inflate contracts and deploy the looted funds to forming political parties as a short cut to political power, and so on.

But these forms of leadership are products of our history and historical experiences.

If we undertake an abridged analysis of the Nigerian predicament today, we can lay the causes of our problems at the roots of colonial and post-colonial dimensions of our history. We can emphasise the distortions and disarticulations of that experience and claim that the leaders that have failed to do much for us are products of an undemocratic, non-accountable, exploitative, repressive, and discriminatory colonial order. Hence, the imperialists systematically produced leaders who would continue in their own ways and left behind structures, institutions, and ideologies that would ensure that departure from the neo-colonial consciousness would be almost impossible without a revolution. Scholars such as Frantz Fanon, Walter Rodney, Aime Cesaire, Claude Ake, and Ade Ajayi have written extensively on the various creative (even if diabolical) ways in which the colonial authorities executed this master plan.

Though not fanciful, this would be an incomplete argument. Unless we wish to lay claim to inferiority and the incapacity to make progress and restructure our inheritances in terms of our own creativity, innovation, and productive energies, it is important that we do not ignore our history. However, we must also make adequate allowances for the post-colonial alignment and realignment of socio-political forces and the interplay of class interests and struggles since political independence in 1960. I believe that we must search elsewhere for the causes or origins of our national *wahala*. While acknowledging the systemic limitations and contradictions, I want to believe that the managers of that system must be carefully examined to understand the level of their culpability. The managers of our system are quite satisfied to blame our failings on colonialism and globalisation as this is a good strategy to cover up their individual and collective incompetence. The failures and failings of the past have squandered the legacy of independence, undermined the present, and mortgaged the future. What is perhaps more frightening is the way in which the current balances of power and policies, especially in the last two decades, have tended to marginalise and discourage genuine leaders while promoting opportunists, charlatans, and mediocrities. Actually, can we say that the majority of our people are better off today than at independence? Have we made much progress since 1960?

It is possible to contend that there is very little *structural* distinction between Nigeria's yesterday and today. This is because the legacies of colonialism and peripheralisation in the global divisions of labour, power, and exchange have continued to shape the character of production, exchange, and consumption, and they remain essentially unaltered even after almost half a century of political independence. From the distortions in the economy and the fragility of the state to the largely unproductive disposition of the power elite and the marginalization of the political economy in the global political economy, not much has changed in Nigeria. We have had reforms, restructurings, minor adjustments here and there, and political epochs but no revolution, effective reformation, or structural transformation.

It is true that we can point at new local governments, new states, new infrastructure, a new national anthem, a new federal capital, new political parties, a new constitution, a wider but not necessarily stronger economy, deeper involvement in the global market due mainly to oil exports, and new discourses on politics and economy. But they have, in large measure and in spite of the civil war, several military juntas, and numerous transitions, been no more than motion in a barber's chair: a lot of movement, but very little progress. Countless opportunities to move forward, restructure and reposition the political economy, and improve the living conditions of the people have been carelessly squandered without apology by the governing elite.

The reality today is that the structural foundations have remained virtually intact. Regional, ethnic, religious, gender, and class suspicions, contradictions, and conflicts continue to deepen by the day. In a nutshell, the custodians of power and politics have failed to improve the quality of leadership and governance or build sustainable foundations for growth, development, and democracy. For things to change, the character of state and class must change. It is only from a democratic and hegemonic state that good governance can flow and positive leadership be provided to the people in their communities and constituencies.

The Nigerian State in Historical Context

True, the Nigerian state is still one in formation. It is quite easy to worry about the rather unfortunate condition of the nation today, but a proper historical understanding of the Nigerian reality can enable any analyst to place our conditions and predicaments in proper context. It is true that the global political economy has been hostile to Nigeria in several ways, but we have failed to initiate structures, institutions, and processes to contain or respond adequately to our extant challenges. We have also failed, like most African states, to take advantage of openings in the global economy to restructure, reform, recompose, and redirect the character of state and class in Nigeria. Even well-intended policies and programmes have been easily undermined by prevailing contradictions, leakages, and conflicts in the system. Our political, social, and economic power blocs have adjusted to the distorted and unproductive system that recycles underdevelopment and crisis. They have persistently shied away from a serious-minded, consistent, and focused structural transformation and repositioning of the political economy. It is therefore not amazing that in spite of Nigerianisation, Africanisation, indigenisation, the war against poverty, Operation Feed the Nation, the Reform Agenda, plans for development, the creation of local governments and states, the oil boom, rolling plans, stabilisation, structural adjustment, and other publicly celebrated strategies, Nigeria is yet to find an answer to any of its numerous challenges. Even good leaders with vision, the few islands of integrity, easily get compromised. Their ideas and achievements are often simply swallowed by a strong and diabolical contraption of indiscipline, political rascality, elite insensitivity, and irresponsibility. No nation on earth has ever made progress in that way.

The Nigerian state on the other hand remains non-hegemonic. Yet, a degree of hegemony is required to maintain the sovereignty of a country, keep the dominant classes under control, maintain an environment that promotes accumulation, and define a nation's location and role in the global system. To be sure, part of the reason for this, aside from the limited hegemony of the state, is the lack of cohesion amongst the ruling or power elite, the distortions in the economy, the vulnerability of the political economy to external interests, and the general condition of poverty in which the majority of Nigerians live. Yet, our elites appear to be disinterested in purposeful and progressive visioning, building state and class hegemony, and establishing viable foundations for holistic progress. In spite of changes in the world, the Nigerian state and its custodians remain rigid in their ideas and politics.

It is amazing how the same names and characters that have done so much damage to our psyche and political values remain influential and in the midst of our power balances and equations. This includes persons who had used their positions to amass wealth illegally, subverted the constitution, and degraded our democratic institutions in the past. They are the same people who have all the access to the seats and structures of power and authority. It is no wonder that the state and its agents find it difficult to move from *government* to *governance*, respect gender equality, structurally transform the foundations of society, distinguish between rulers and leaders, and refocus the nation for sustained progress.

The basis of Nigeria's leadership failure can be found in its concentration in largely unproductive but lucrative and quick revenue-generating ventures. We have a lot of people with cash capital but with very little capitalist drive or initiative. They are traders, speculators, consultants, (foreign) manufacturers' representatives, and commercialists. Such a class has never built a sustainable economy or polity. In addition, the state is the primary means of accumulation. Until the accumulative base shifts from the state or public treasury and speculation to investment in technology, research, ideas, and real *production*, the leaders can only be superficial and opportunistic.

The power elite appears to have a pathological fixation on subverting the foundations of the state, collaborating with undemocratic forces to abridge democratic rights, and designing dubious and diabolical strategies to close political spaces, suffocate civil society, enthrone a culture of anti-intellectualism, and rusticate opportunities and possibilities for progress and development. Until recently, the culture and obsession of the power elite was on building a parallel or alternate state at the expense of the public good. In its failure, it has created private alternatives in the following areas:

Water – private boreholes rather than public water systems.

Health services – private and foreign hospitals in place of general or public hospitals.

Schools for children – expensive private schools in and outside the country at the expense of public schools

Security – private bodyguards and security systems rather than collective or community and public security.

Electricity – private generators as against public electricity supply.

Foreign travel – use of foreign rather than national airlines, vacations abroad rather than local alternatives

Banking stolen funds – Though stealing is bad, even then they patronize foreign banks. Their counterparts do not even consider Nigerian banks for this purpose.

Houses or homes as "prisons" – high walls, complex security gadgets, electrified fences, huge dogs, closed-circuit televisions, etc. – more defended than local prisons!

How can a country move forward when the elite, the leaders, the very custodians of state power, those who ought to set the example and give hope and inspiration, act as if they have themselves lost faith in the present and future of their own nation? How can the nation have a future when the elite appears to be turning its back on the nation? Now, just as happened in Ghana, Senegal, South Africa, the elite are buying designer houses in Brazil and Dubai and taking pride in their foreign assets. Where they can help it, they die in foreign hospitals and then we are told that they died with one white doctor by their bedside! These are not the type of leaders who take time to think of how to deepen democratic values and practices; and they cannot be relied upon to be apostles of good governance.

What is more painful is that this same elite presided over the squandering of trillions of naira, ran down our basic institutions – Eleme Petrochemicals, Nigeria Airways, the Oku Iboku paper mill, Nigeria Shipping Lines, the legendary refineries, the Nicon-Hilton hotel, Nigeria Coal Corporation, all government catering rest houses, all government printing presses, Ajaokuta Steel, Delta Steel, NIOMCO, the various ports, Nigeria Railways, and so on. The list is embarrassingly long. How can we build a future on such a gargantuan display of fiscal recklessness, administrative rascality and incompetence, and managerial mediocrity?

To hide the extent to which they have compromised our future, they try to legitimate corruption, manipulate primordial differences, and exaggerate socio-cultural differences. They divert attention to non-issues by creating all sorts of ethnic and counter-ethic associations and pretend to be using them to defend the interests of the people. They exhibit a criminal fixation on the capture of raw power by all means necessary including violence, thuggery, lies, bribery, the stuffing of ballot boxes, the exclusion of candidates from the ballot, the manipulation of security forces, and even the use of *juju*! The power they spend so much to grab is not for the promotion or advancement of peace, stability, basic human needs, or progress, but for the enhancement of primitive accumulation, the reproduction of underdevelopment, and the recycling of undemocratic conduct. They are not interested in intellectual discourses, which they often dismiss as nothing but "grammar"! You hardly ever find them reading newspapers, and most have not read a book in many years!

Somehow, the leadership and governance question is complicated by the seeming acquiescence of the people as they continue to hero-worship discredited and disgraced "leaders" in society. They receive traditional titles, are honoured by churches, receive national honours and awards, and are praised in songs by musicians. Many of the poor, their consciousness already dampened and weakened by neglect, manipulation, and abuse, have simply decided to follow the gravy train of bad governance and contaminated leadership.

It is, however, instructive that the islands of integrity and courage in society have continued to serve as the face of opposition even at great cost. They have continued to ask new questions, insist on merit, fair play, accountability, social justice, and sensitivity to the plight of the ordinary person. They insist that the only way to promote good governance and accountable leadership is to reject those who have been tainted in the past, who are now running around as leaders, decision-makers, democrats, and godfathers They argue that new standards must be set for identifying and supporting those with leadership qualities that will serve individual, national, and collective interests. Finally, they insist that good governance, democracy, and responsible leadership cannot thrive if all Nigerians do not take a firm stand against election rigging, the abuse of power, the subversion of the constitution, the manipulation of public policies, and the enthronement of mediocrity in our national life.

The Leadership Challenge in Nigeria

For the late President Umaru Musa Yar'Adua, the Nigerian predicament could be put squarely as the challenge of leadership. As he put it, the "concept of leadership has been bastardised in Nigeria, and people use leadership positions to show arrogance, oppress others and misappropriate resources meant for the generality of Nigerians instead of serving them as directed by God" (*Leadership,* August 1, 2008, p. 3). While the late president was absolutely correct, the fact remains that these leaders operate within a system that encourages impunity, the abuse of office, rascality, and indiscipline. These same people work at very high and prestigious positions internationally, and they never abuse their offices or misbehave. However, once they are given opportunities within Nigeria, they begin to do all that the president had referred to and worse. This means that we must look again at the structures and institutions of the state, the constitution, the character of policy making, the enforcement of laid-down rules and regulations, political will, and the involvement of the people in politics and policy to fully appreciate why leadership is what it is or has turned out to be. Is it not amazing that all the numerous reports on the Niger Delta since 1956 have recommended virtually the same solutions but not one of these recommendations has been implemented? Is this just insensitivity, political rascality, or plain wickedness – to leave communities and constituencies, fellow Nigerians whose land produces so much wealth, in grinding poverty and environments that resemble worse than the Fourth World! How do we explain the existence of thousands of abandoned projects all over the country today? What is the explanation for thousands of dilapidated schools, hospitals, and public institutions around Nigeria? Why do our so-called leaders measure their wealth, success, and importance with the degree of poverty around them? How do we account for children hawking in dangerous traffic when they should be in school? Why has the looting of public funds become almost institutionalised and yet we cannot find any of the hundreds of arrested or prosecuted looters in any prison? Every so often we read in the newspapers of persons being declared "wanted". However, very few ever get as far as the courts, and even fewer ever get any punishment. The implication is that the system has been structured to encourage corruption in the knowledge that nothing will happen.

Because leadership in Nigeria has been largely pedestrian, opportunistic, unpatriotic, and insensitive to the plight of the people, it is still possible to see regionalized or ethnic-based agendas whether it is *Afenifere, Ohaneze, Arewa,* the Northern Union, the South-South People's Assembly, or the like. It is the failure of elite and state hegemony that encourages primordialism and parochialism. In fact, where the state is seen as largely irrelevant to the survival of the ordinary citizen, coping or survival mechanisms are invented and become routine. This eats away at the capacity and capability of the state to perform the basic function of government, much less that of a state. On the other hand, coping mechanisms congeal divisive political and cultural enclaves based on ethnicity, region, gender, religion, profession or atavism. Loyalty is transferred from a state that is seen as repressive, already captured by a few, and "irrelevant" to other non-repressive organisations and outlets for social expression. This is why we have prominent ethnic and regional rather than truly *national* leaders today. And this is why everything that we do in Nigeria is evaluated through the lenses of religious, regional, and ethnic considerations.

These trends and tendencies of distrust and covert and/or overt opposition are expressed in the numerous coalitions, contradictions, conflicts, and confusions in society. There is hardly a consensus on any issue in Nigeria, including the continued survival and unity of the country. This in itself is a sad and unfortunate development after the Nigerian civil war and the high price that was paid by our fellow citizens. Indeed, between and within economic, cultural, political, and social communities and constituencies, the degree of distrust remains very heavy and deep. University graduates and HND holders are at war; NECO and WAEC certificate holders are treated differently; so-called career and non-career officers are at war; north and south, Niger-delta versus the rest of the nation, and security and non-security personnel are not communicating. Within the Nigerian Christian community, the competition and commercialisation have gone beyond rational understanding. Within universities, cultists and non-cultists are at war. Libraries are either empty or over a decade behind in relevant literature and journals, and many academics are involved in general business and consulting rather than serious research and teaching. In addition, rural and urban dwellers, the poor and the rich, landlords and tenants, employed and unemployed, and segments or sectors of the private sector strive to outdo and undo each other as opportunity permits. Nothing seems to go in an orderly or predictable manner. Recruitment into paramilitary forces results in the death of several applicants. Satellites get lost in space within a few years of purchase and launching, while airplanes disappear for months only to be found by farmers, despite the billions invested in emergency rescue and satellites! In the midst of all these events, we have leaders – mostly self-imposed leaders – who have simply refused or failed to lead us anywhere. Today, in 2010, we are still discussing the very same problems and challenges that dominated national discourses at independence in 1960: education, power, industry, security, healthcare delivery, and agriculture, especially food production.

Is it any wonder, therefore, that legislators who are asked to probe corruption end up being probed themselves? Trust, accommodation, and cooperation exist in hardly any aspect of national life. As public institutions crumble or give the façade of a beautiful existence based on their architectural outlays, within the institutions there exist oceans of conflict, waste, manipulation, oppression, indiscipline, arrogance of power, ethnic jingoism, and downright terrorisation of the powerless and those with no godfathers or political connections. While the judiciary has remained the longest undisturbed arm of government in spite of numerous assaults especially by the military juntas over the years, it has also not escaped the rot in the system. Some judicial judgments leave many lawyers wondering if so-called non-learned persons have invaded the sector, not to mention countless allegations of bribery made against judges at all levels. Of course, these are all manifestations of the structural deformities in the system and the rather unsteady constitution of the non-hegemonic state under the control of a badly factionalised and fractionalised leadership. In this context, the followers take strategic but reactionary positions on the political landscape and use their own hands to destroy their environment and foul up the system. The entire nation suffers while the so-called leaders subsidise and lubricate their survival with looted public funds and monies in foreign banks. While others wallow in poverty, frustration, and uncertainty, the leaders keep their families abroad and their children in super luxury apartments and expensive foreign schools, with enough resources to travel around the world.

Why do the Nigerian state and its custodians find it so difficult to move in one direction so that our people can conserve and deploy their individual and collective energy for productive purposes? The time and energy that we waste in traffic, looking for essential necessities, and just trying to survive bad roads, the lack of power, and other pressures are enough to transform a society. How is Nigeria going to move forward in the midst of plan indiscipline, policy inconsistency, competitive rather than complementary programmes, the duplication of services and functions, and the re-awarding of the same contract over and over again even by the same government? How can we move forward with empty libraries and laboratories, poor research culture, limited concern for futurology and visioning, and an inability to identify and use the best brains and hands in the larger society? We must begin to think out of the box and break out of the barber's chair of motion without progress. If the leaders, after almost fifty years, refuse to lead, the people and their organisations must bypass them.

Let us look briefly at leadership at the political level. Nigerians at home and abroad are very familiar with the political abracadabra that has been foisted on the nation in the name of politics, party registration and re-registration, nominations, primaries, and elections. In spite of the existence of a constitution, political parties, and party rules and regulations, politics is war in Nigeria. It is therefore easy to understand why many Nigerians wept and celebrated the victory of Obama in faraway America. In fact, a former president of the country once described politics, and elections in particular, as a "do or die" affair. Politics are costly, diabolical, unsteady, and uncertain, and announced results hardly ever reflect what took place on election day. It is not unusual for political leaders to ambush and undermine the best candidates before or during the primaries. Only in a few cases are the best candidates presented for political office, and aspirants are almost bankrupted before they get elected. This in itself lays the foundation for the arrogance of power, executive recklessness, and unbridled corruption. Until our political parties become truly and fully reformed, Nigeria cannot move forward. Until the parties begin to respect their own rules, Nigeria cannot produce credible, capable, courageous, and visionary leaders who will build the political economy and consolidate democratic institutions and practices. The parties must begin to perform some of the basic functions of political parties – identify and train leaders, develop policy platforms, present the best aspirants and candidates for office, regulate office holders, sanction erring members, monitor office holders, conduct research on party and political development, encourage public discourses, and commit openly to the sustenance of democracy in every regard. I am not aware of any political party in Nigeria today that is carrying out these important functions.

Office holders that emerge from a dubious and diabolical process cannot be expected to respect the constitution or liberties. They cannot be expected to distinguish between the public and private treasury. They cannot provide responsible leadership or preach the gospel of democracy to the populace. Obviously, political manipulations in the struggle for power and the absence of internal democracy within political parties establish a negative basis for building leadership, good governance, and democratic values. That is why we must never tire of the struggle for democratic practices and social justice. Political parties in Nigeria must be bastions of fair play, justice, and freedom. Unless this happens, they will be contributing directly to the consolidation and reproduction of poverty, insecurity, and underdevelopment in Nigeria. The practice of writing names rather than going to the primaries, unjustly disqualifying aspirants for mundane and inexplicable reasons, favouring minions, relatives, and associates without attention to qualifications, and amending the rules of the game just to satisfy selfish interests must be jettisoned if ever Nigeria is to produce credible leaders who can stand the test of time.

This is exactly why electoral reforms to correct the defects of our present system are more than urgent in Nigeria. This will ensure the efficient and speedy adjudication of critical petitions, the careful monitoring of electoral processes by civil society groups, and severe sanctions for all electoral offences. It is one of the strategic ways to get our politics rights, and when this happens, we can get our economic directions right. We require focused and capable leaders to ensure that politics is no longer seen as a business, an opportunity to loot the treasury and mortgage the future of our dear country. The reformed electoral process will ensure the emergence of the right institutions and the right candidates who in turn will nurture an appropriate environment for democracy and development.

The constitution review process, which ought to enable the country to address some existing socioeconomic and political fault lines, has turned into an opportunity to pick fights, quarrel over procedures, squander scarce resources, and engage in distractions and diversions. The very last effort was contaminated and destroyed by the narrow interests of a few at the expense of the common good. So, we threw out the baby, the bathwater and even the basin. We lost everything. Billions of naira went down the drain, no questions asked. Today, we are starting all over. This is not one man's show, and it must not be an ego trip. It is not the senators versus the representatives. It is not the National Assembly versus the rest of the nation. Rather, it is one more golden chance to give ourselves a *living* document, a true people's covenant, a roadmap to show us how to organise and deploy power in the collective interests of our people. It is an opportunity to correct historical injustices against women, the youth, the poor, micro-minorities, and minorities. It is an opportunity to stop oil theft, kidnapping, illegal bunkering, arson, assassinations, money laundering, hostage taking, and other forms of violence in the much neglected and exploited Niger Delta by providing the right context for political engagements, institution building, policy making, and leadership development. It is an opportunity to produce the document that will engender peace, stability, dialogue, tolerance, diversity, unity, democracy, and progress in Nigeria.

I doubt this will happen if the process remains opportunistic, elitist, and complicated. We must draw lessons from Uganda, South Africa, Eritrea, Ghana, and other parts of the world by adopting a truly open, consultative, transparent, accountable, process-driven, and people-driven approach to constitution-making. This is the only way to produce a constitution that we can all understand, own, and defend with our lives. This is the way to build the architecture to deepen, widen, promote, sustain, and reproduce democracy and democratization. The process of refederalisation will be possible and much more viable with a true constitutional consultation and process that brings our people together and restructures our political compact. It is also the only way to build a culture of constitutionalism; the process publicises it, mobilises the people, and wins buy-in from them. If we do not get the politics right, we can never get our development right. Political uncertainty, contradictions, distrust, violence, and instability will continue to challenge well-intentioned programmes and policies and thus reproduce underdevelopment and bad leadership. Given the challenges of growth and development in Nigeria today, this is not the time to fight over chairmanship versus deputy or vice-chairmanship or even the right to amend the constitution. Just involve the people, provide leadership, and let the open process flow.

The failure of leaders, especially in the formal sphere, has increased the relevance of ethnic leaders, militants, and primordial warlords. Of course, the masses themselves live as if under a spell. Disappointed by regime after regime, government after government, and leader after leader, they give obedience on the surface, more to avoid oppression and death than out of loyalty, love, or patriotism. Their souls have been so mangled and corrupted that they have nothing but cynicism and disregard for the state, the custodians of power, and state policies. They have adopted coping and survival mechanisms to make it through the confusion and uncertainty in which they find themselves. To get any service from government agencies, they first prepare the bribe, then the required fee. They know that if they do not do so, there is no chance on earth that they would get any service – job application, national passport, driver's licence, import licence, building permit, vehicle licence, tax clearance, national ID card, you name it. Many have retreated into community, ethnic, religious, and other demonic and occult enclaves as they hope endlessly for political rationality, sensitive leadership, and adequate democratic spaces in which to survive. In other instances, Nigerians abuse the name of God, as the Almighty is invoked at the slightest opportunity even while perpetrating evil against individuals, community, and the entire nation. A few have designed ways to use religion, especially Christianity, to get rich and further impoverish the already poor. It is no wonder that one can find twenty branches of the same church or denomination worshipping the same Almighty on a single street in most of our major cities! Only recently have some church leaders come to declare that fasting and prayers cannot change Nigeria. For the most part, where is the leadership from the religious leaders? It is not enough to speak after every religious clash. Prevention is better than lamentation!

The "elasticity of hope" in Nigeria is just incredible. In spite of the rascality, corruption, arrogance, insensitivity, and socio-economic violence unleashed on the majority by the minority power elite, a revolution has not taken place, even if anger and disillusionment often result in pockets of open resistance. Hope is almost becoming the opium of the Nigerian: *e go beta*, *God dey*, "tomorrow will be better", "when my child grows up I will eat my share of the cake", are used to rationalise tolerance for bad leadership, corruption, and bad governance. Nigerians must learn to shake off fatalistic and opportunistic rationalisations for the leadership failure in Nigeria.

How All These Relate to Good Governance

Governance refers to the structural and institutional arrangements in society that shape production, politics, and accumulation. It is the basis of social and political security, the contestation for power, the management of conflicts, and the construction of the overall political and administrative architecture of society. Such arrangements can be good or bad. These arrangements are bad when on the average they are not deployed towards the systematic and structural changes that move a society closer to meeting the basic human needs of the majority: this is bad governance. The indicators of governance are rather easy to understand, and there are universal standards for measurement: education (literacy), levels of child and maternal mortality, gainful employment, infrastructure development to facilitate better living, affordable housing for the people, a sustainable environment, gender equality, the availability of affordable food, access to healthcare delivery, the availability of potable water, social security, civil liberties, and the opportunity to participate in decision making at any desired level. Of course, the deliverables in these areas are dependent on the character of politics, leadership, and the context of politics and policy making.

Applied to Nigeria, as discussed in earlier portions of this paper, can we say that our policy makers, politicians, and leaders at all levels have worked hard to produce a society that is fair to all? Can we conclude that our economic indicators – especially employment, food production, economic diversity, food availability, inflation rates, and so on – are aggregated on the side of the majority and more than half of our people are enjoying a better life? Are the rules of politics, economy, exchange, and consumption respected by all as established? Is the investment climate predictable and reliable? Are we making headway in poverty eradication and the reduction of social stress amongst the populace? Is the battle against corruption achieving its objectives and sanctioning culprits? Are citizens secure and free from violence? Are public institutions efficient, effective, transparent, accountable, and result-oriented? Can we conclude that the rule of law, civil liberties, social justice, access to justice, the distribution of resources on an equitable basis, and the freedom to participate in free and fair elections the basis of our collective existence and engagements in Nigeria? The answer is in the negative.

The implication here is that the governance environment in Nigeria is negative and hostile and only allows bad leadership to thrive. Good leaders are a rare breed and are an endangered species at all times in contemporary Nigeria. In its total package, it is impossible to declare that good governance operates in Nigeria. Where bad leadership and bad governance converge, the result is usually the uncertainty, instability, inefficiency, violence, corruption, and underdevelopment that we witness in Nigeria.

Out from the Ashes: Leadership and the Future

So, in conclusion, what brand of leaders do we need in Nigeria? No one can deny the positive value of good leadership to a family, business, community, or nation. Even religious bodies and NGOs cannot thrive without good leadership. This is because good, accountable, efficient, effective, sensitive, and God-fearing leadership brings hope, courage, and peace, and encourages productivity, creativity, and innovation.

Good leadership builds bridges and bonds of tolerance, inclusion, pluralism, love, friendship, and partnership. Good leadership helps people to bear the pains of setbacks while inspiring the generality to reach the highest points of their productive and creative abilities. Good leadership is pro-people, especially the youth, women, and the physically challenged. It is pro-community, pro-environmental protection, pro-social justice, pro-accountability, and pro-democracy in disposition. We have lived through all brands of leadership in Nigeria, and we all know the opposite of good leadership. The consequences, pains, frustrations, and embarrassment of bad leadership, at times quite demonic in its manifestation, are there for all to see. This means that we cannot afford to continue to test the waters, give another chance to known crooks, accommodate incompetence, experiment with perpetual underachievers, tolerate persons that have no respect for the people and communities, consider persons with no democratic credentials, and give them room, by acts of omission or commission, to toy with our present and future again. We must remember, as one young African leader put it recently, that "one year of bad leadership can take us back ten to twenty years. In other words, one year of bad leadership can contaminate and destroy ten solid years of progress."

The leaders that we choose at all levels and sectors must not be those who will undermine democracy, terrorise society, loot the treasury, build their own mansions, and keep their own children abroad while making life hell on earth for the majority. We must pick leaders who value education, industrialization, infrastructural development, capacity building, and information and communication technology. We must pick leaders who understand globalization and "glocalization", leaders who know the value of environmental protection and understand that health is wealth. We must set the local, sub-structural, and internal facilities, policies, and programmes in place appropriately so that investors will come on their own rather than making daily runs around the globe at huge public cost in search of investors that we never see. Once we restructure our society, strengthen structures of accountability and service delivery, have the right leaders in place, and feed and employ our people, we will have fully re-branded our country. Tourists and investors will come on their own accord or with little motivation.

Our leaders, with all due respect, must have education, exposure, experience, competence, vision, integrity, dignity, commitment, and moral depth. They must have compassion, sensitivity, a track record of service, and identification with the people. They must be capable of favouring accountability, transparency, due process, and service delivery. Our leaders of the future must be God-fearing, morally sound, spiritually confident, credible, honest, reliable, progressive, and with a sense of mission and a sense of *nation.* Their loyalty must be to the state and not to a godfather, some shrine, or a hidden bank account. Their commitment to uplifting the conditions of the people, rehabilitating our dilapidated infrastructure and institutions, empowering communities and constituencies, and building lasting bonds of friendship and partnership across ethnic, religious, regional, and gender lines must be absolute.

The leaders we identify and select to manage our lives, resources, and future must have courage to admit mistakes, correct errors, alter our decadent past, build new opportunities, support radical ideas, attract investments, and bring our nation at par with the rest of the world in every way. Nigeria's future leaders must know Nigeria and the world.

In this era of globalization and instant information, we cannot afford to tolerate ignoramuses, people who hate reading, and those who would rather die than think. Our leaders must understand and appreciate good governance as the foundation of social justice, the rule of law, equity, popular participation, mobilisation, and sustainable development. Good governance enhances patriotism, honesty, new leadership, and unity because it puts the people at the core of politics, policies, and social actions. Our new leaders must be humble but tough, caring without being careless, and loving without being stupid.

Finally, our new leaders must be persons who can appreciate the beauty of our communities and country, the sacrifices of our past heroes and heroines, the central place of women in our national development, the boundless energy of our youth, the productivity and energy of our workers, the indomitable spirit of our armed forces, the creativity of our traders, the strength of character of our traditional and religious leaders, and the innocence, purity, and smiles of our babies, who invariably represent our boundless future.

Chapter Four
EXCELLENCE AS A MORAL VISION FOR POLITICAL LEADERSHIP
Nimi Wariboko

Introduction

Politics is ultimately about living well, men and women living well in the *common*. The political is "the site where being in common is at stake", and "having access to what is proper to existence, and therefore, of course, to the proper of one's own existence."[1] Thus, all political actions (words and deeds) are really about our being-in-common; and what is always at stake in this *in-between* where we are *ex-posed* to one another is the character of possibilities of life. Always and above all this boils down to actualization of potentialities of both individuals and community. And the moral vision that undergirds it is simply this: to live best in accordance with the best of ourselves, as Aristotle once said.

Ancient Greek philosophers used the word *arête* to describe a thing or function that is done well. For instance, the *arête* of a knife is to cut and cut very well. The *arête* of leadership is about the well-being of the persons in a given community in accordance with the supreme principle of the community.

This paramount principle was either about playing one part well in the cosmic order of duties and roles or moving toward full actualization of individual potentialities, the flourishing life (*eudaimonia*). The moral act for the Greeks was not merely an act done well, but one done with the appropriate motives and the appropriate knowledge.

Arête is usually translated into English as virtue, excellence, or moral excellence. In Greek thought, the attainment of *arête* is part of the movement of human beings as they go from potency to act according to their mode of being and operation. A careful analysis of the ancient understanding of *arête* will easily reveal that *arête*, excellence, means striving for the creative realization of human potentialities, the paradigmatic virtue the exercise of which leads to the achievement of human flourishing.[2]

This notion of politics as a purpose-driven campaign to develop human and communal capabilities is not alien to our traditional political philosophy. First, the well-being of the community is the paramount moral value of all persons in the community in all its spheres of life. If the preservation of the community's well-being is the highest good for which all should seek in all actions, it is then the complete end "for the sake of which the other things are done."[3] One needs to add that the paramount community virtue is not just concerned with community well-being. The concern for the community's well-being is simultaneously a concern for what the individual person can *do* and *be* if such a person is not limited. There is the belief that every individual has been endowed by God (or gods) with certain gifts to bless his or her community, and the community needs to help the individual to fully realize this potential.

In this essay, I want to address excellence as a moral vision for political leadership in Nigeria. This is to say our task is to investigate the nature of leadership driven by a deep and abiding orientation to the creation of the good community and dynamic transformation of humanity based on the principle of excellence. My thesis is that the urgent project of Nigeria's national development calls for actualization of the potentialities of all her citizens and the principle of excellence supplies the necessary logic and power for it.

The rest of this essay will proceed in the following manner. First, I will address what the orientation and commitment to excellence means in political leadership. Second, I will show its implication for understanding and politically managing the task of national economic development. Third, we will discuss what excellence on a daily basis means for political leaders. A summary and conclusion follows as the last section.

Politics of Excellence

The challenge and invitation of excellence as a moral vision for national development is how to create the politics, *eros*,[4] and ethos in our communities so that every person will actualize to the highest level possible his or her potentialities. All this has implications for the way we approach the management of our community (local, state, or national) and its common good. At the minimum, excellence in communal governance practice will involve the creation of possibilities for community and participation by all its members so that their potentialities can be drawn out for the common good. A community should be adjudged good because it allows its people to develop their potentialities in the pursuit of an ever-greater common good. How well a community does this will depend on how it allows individuals to develop their unique traits, capabilities, and potentialities and on how well these individual endowments are related to each other in the pursuit of the common good. An excellent community is one that is adept at combining these two opposite tendencies or processes: a movement toward uniqueness counterbalanced by a movement toward union.

In such a community the orientation toward the *not-yet* permeates all of its social practices and individual lives. The goal of politics is to create possibilities for all to participate in the polity and to realize their potentialities and in so doing to enable the community to realize its potentialities. Science is an engagement with nature so as to fully understand, realize, extend, and create possibilities buried in the potentialities of all beings and processes in the universe. Education (*e-ducere*) is to draw out and lead forth the potentialities of a person. The organization of market competition is also oriented in this way – it is *agonistic*. The Latin root of our English word "competition" is *conpetire*, which means to seek together. In competition the participants help each other to stretch their skills as each meets the challenge posed by the other. What each participant is seeking is the actualization of his or her own most potential and to help the other person come to his or her best.[5] In the same vein, an excellent friendship is the type of partnership and fellowship in which each person aspires to bring to realization the latent potentialities of the other. The friends say to another, "Let your actualization advance as mine does." An individual's life will be adjudged excellent if it is a life that is engaged in the pursuit of ever greater development and creative realization of his or her potentials. This involves, among other endeavours, overcoming challenges to create, manage, and sustain possibilities for responsible personal development.

In this light, one major task of political leadership is to direct thinking on how to develop the best society for releasing of potentialities of all persons and institutions for the common good and for human flourishing. Alternatively put, the object of the political leader is to create a society that is not only attuned to possibilities for full development of potentialities, but that also enjoys excellence. Taking one's stance in excellence is one veritable way of calling into account all of society's institutions, laws, religions, relationships, and the like. Do they facilitate the release of potentialities and the creation of new (alternative) possibilities for a more perfect human flourishing or do they require the suppression of them? Those which fail this test deserve to be set aside. The leader is also to evaluate all emerging possibilities, amidst the range of all present possibilities, so as to project the direction of human flourishing of a particular community in relation to his or her sense of what its citizens want to become.

Based on this understanding of political leadership, politics is a way of being for excellence, a way of being for human flourishing. One does not value human flourishing as one should if one does not care about excellence (the persistent creative realizations of human potentialities) for its own sake.[6] This way of thinking of politics is against the grain of modern "bureaucratic" thinking on politics.

Contemporary political science has settled comfortably into the technocratic management of society (economy). The constant and reliable has come to dominate the novel and the dynamic. In the technocratic conception of politics, faith in the power of political subject is not faith in a revolutionary event. Politics, in fact, is only a negative assertion: the social order does not die, it does not change. In a non-technocratic conception, politics is a positive assertion: the whole system, which has really died a thousand deaths by exclusions and marginalization, is (or can be) resurrected by a new act of creation orchestrated by the agent(s) subject to the good, truth, and beauty of excellence.[7] Today, politics is no longer about re-membering the social order or developing a new structure for justice. Politics has long passed the era when it was about starting a new *praxis* from a point (or moments) of social dysfunction in the system in order to move society to an alternative path. Alas, it is no longer about unfolding being as a consequence of subjects' decisions about liberating and life-enhancement potentials, but it is all about positing being as a manipulation of institutional and bureaucratic practices. Politics is no longer about encountering the *real*. Modern political science has inaugurated a forgetting of *real* behind current forms of sociality and behind all sources of new solution.

But we must re-understand politics as the possibility of change in every social order – insofar as change is understood as an openness to the "unfinishedness" of life and the emergence of new alternatives. In doing this, we must not reject the management orientation of politics, but we have to redefine and expand it to incorporate the management of novelty and concentration on possibility for perpetual orientation to the *good* of excellence, the enrichment of life. The pursuit of this good must not be totally severed from a transcendent source or norm as such a move can become a serious threat to life or the being-in-common.

The state is not an agent without character and principles, improvising its decisions or governance. It must be committed to respecting the inherent human dignity and equality of all citizens (as bearers of God's image and endowed with the right and duty to participate in the common good) and creating the conditions of possibility necessary for safeguarding human dignity. Such a state will not act in ways that block the unfolding of potentialities and the promises of God in the lives of persons or social groups within and outside its borders.

Excellence and Economic Development

To demonstrate how the ethical framework of excellence I am proposing in this essay can help move the discourse on economic underdevelopment, a well-known hindrance to human flourishing and excellence, I will engage the development theory of Nobel Prize winning economist Amartya Sen. I extend his theory of *development as freedom* in new directions so as to locate it in the construct of excellence.[8] The result is that I put forward a new philosophical perspective on economic development –that of *development as excellence*. Excellence is an "opening" that allows economic development to manifest itself, and it is what is behind the search for economic *freedoms* as human capability development.

The overall purpose here is to analyse how an understanding of the concept of excellence will impact our thinking about economic development. What kind of light will be shed on Sen's notion of development as *freedom*? He has argued that economic development is not just about quantitative increases in gross national product, but principally about giving people the freedoms, the *capabilities* to become both the means (agents) and the end (goals and recipients) of their own economic development. Bringing this about, he argues, involves deliberate successive removal and vigilant resistance to *unfreedoms*.

Particularly, Sen has famously described economic development as *freedom*. By this he means the continuous and calculated attempt to remove *unfreedoms*, endowing people with capabilities so that they will become both the agents (means) and end of their economic development process. I find two major shortcomings in his analysis. First, the idea of development as freedom is not philosophically linked to humans who have the "future in their being". Humans are by nature future-oriented and we need to know how the constant struggle to eliminate *unfreedoms* is related to their basic nature. Second, there is no discussion of the basic ontological foundation of freedom. Is the human struggle to create and sustain freedom – of which economic development is just one major aspect – basic to what it means to be human? What is it about human beings that may possibly undergird the search for freedom? In this essay, I argue that what undergirds economic development and its aim of freedom is excellence. Excellence is the matrix from which freedoms come forth. So I will argue for a new perspective in economic development: *development as excellence*. This is not to say that economic development and excellence are identical, and I am not positing that we should think of excellence only in terms of economic development, only within the territory of developed countries, or even only in terms of scientific-technological breakthrough. I believe that material economic development can never be the ground and essence of excellence, but excellence can flash in its manifestation in the dimension of development or scientific-technological breakthrough.

As already noted above, Sen has made a fine distinction between economic development as increase in total output and economic development as *freedom*. He writes about development as *freedom*; development is presented as release from *unfreedoms*, as the veritable engine (agent, cause) of development. I interpret this notion of freedom as the dynamic quality of human existence. Freedom as an agent of development points beyond itself, demanding for its completion in further progress. Development (rising gross national product) itself points beyond itself, also demanding more development, more unshackling from *unfreedoms*. But the nature of the demand for completion is different in each case. When economic development points beyond itself, to demand completion, it is about the filling in of what is lacking in human well-being. We add what we consider to be lacking to our basic well-being. Electricity, education, and medical services, for example, are added to complete the incomplete life of dehumanizing (incomplete) existence. "Such is the case, for example, with the restoration of a mutilated statue, of a partially destroyed painting. We see the need for completion, see too in what general direction it points; by supplying what has been missing, we make the incomplete complete."[9]

But when economic development as freedom demands completion, when it points beyond itself, it is not about filling or adding, but is strictly about replacing. The demand for completion of every gain of freedom "is not only toward the appearance of something that is not yet [more freedoms], but at the same time toward the disappearance of what is now present."[10] For example, the state of incompleteness, the absence of an adequate capability to properly weigh and trade agricultural produce on the part of an illiterate village woman expresses itself in the demand for education. The demand for education would not be satisfied (the inability to weigh properly would not go away) if a government measuring agency were simply provided to her. The appearance of the proper skills of measurement demands for the disappearance of illiteracy. For the education to be a complete freedom, illiteracy must disappear. What is lacking must appear in the place of what is given. In economic development as quantitative increment, what was lacking now appears besides the lack, but in development as freedom, what was lacking succeeds to take the place of the lack. As Victor Zuckerkandl put it in his comparison of visual incompleteness and auditory incompleteness in music, "The demand for completion on the part of a tone is a demand to cease being and to let something else, something that is not yet, appear."[11]

What is common to both cases (freedom and material quantitative development) is the "something dynamic, the pointing beyond itself, a demand for completion",[12] and this common basis is excellence. Excellence is the dynamic that undergirds economic development either as an addition to the current level of well-being or as the generator of freedoms that must necessarily displace *unfreedoms*. This common basis needs to be investigated and properly understood by economists, but it has been largely ignored. I find the neglect of this basic human dynamic in the general debate toward defining economic development unacceptable.

Economists have interpreted economic development with the purpose of delivering it. With a few notable exceptions, this concern has been limited to making (creating, engineering) development and not with understanding it. To put it in a rather gross comparison: the problems of economists are the problems of composition rather than of music. What they have mainly said is all about the difficult technique of producing development. There is nothing much to hang on to when it comes to understanding development itself, its nature, and its essence. Development must be properly related to human nature in all of its physical, social, and spiritual dimensions via excellence. All this is not intended as a blame or reproach but to point out that there is a need to understand the inner core of development. In other words, how can economic ethics, philosophy, or theology of development focus on the problems of electricity rather than on the problems of the electrician, to use Zuckerkandl's analogy.[13] In this study, I want to ask and address the questions that are internal to the development phenomenon.

Both economists and ethicists appear not to be focused on the inner core of development. Some of them need to play the role of the nineteenth-century English physicist Michael Faraday to understand the "electricity" of economic development, and others need to play the role of Hollywood technicians who set up the neon lights to dazzle people. But this is not happening. Economists and ethicists are arguing against each other from the same side of the fence. A third voice is needed to both enrich the flow of the debate and nudge it away from the eddy in which it is trapped. Economists say development – no matter how it is sliced and diced – conveys the sense of a series of gains in well-being, flourishing. Ethicists argue that it is the positive changes in well-being that make a series of steps in innovations, inventions, and transformations meaningful. This writer would suggest that a series of innovations or growths in gross domestic product will no more make the essence of development than successions of tones will make a melody. "A melody is a series of tones that makes sense."[14] Strictly speaking, melody and rhythm happen in between the tones.[15] It happens in the "margin", and this is useful knowledge to have. As we will see below in this essay, excellence happens in the margin too.

At first blush, it may appear that ethicists and neoclassical economists differ greatly on the idea of economic development. The debate between neoclassical economists and ethicists is not about the succession of progress that marks development but the *meaning* in the progress. Yet neither meaning nor succession is at the inner core of development. What is it then that adheres in a succession of progress? Or what adheres in the changes in meaning of the series of material and immaterial gains that is at the core of what it means to be developing in general? In all these there is a pointing toward – every movement is dictating a direction, placing itself in a direction, wants to pass beyond itself, and does not want itself.[16] This is in the nature of all succession, and every take on development consciously or unconsciously presupposes it. Thus, no series of progress, no amount of changes in ethical meaning, and no interpretation of economic progress is capable of making a good conclusion. The dynamic quality that accrues (attends) to human existence is the inner core of development. It is this inner core that encompasses and transcends every form of economic development that I have been investigating in this essay.

This dynamic quality is properly the human quality of development. It is a universal quality of the finite being, the concrete actuality of being called human. It is a universal dimension of human existence. This dynamic quality is in a certain sense what makes us human and undergirds the development process. This demand to proceed, this unfinishedness of every step that accrues to every activity, to every meaning in the context of existence is integral to what it means to be human. It is a process in which a human becomes a person and ceases to be a "thing."[17]

It is the original fact and act of every self-creativity and self-transcendence. The dynamic self-realization, self-affirmation is a fundamental character of human life. It gives validity to every development, and it is present in every development or progress. In every progress, innovation, invention, or transformation, the human personhood actualizes itself. This dynamic quality of human existence can be analysed philosophically or theologically – philosophically only if we examine it just as it is, but theologically if we also affirm it as a manifestation of the infinite or show how it can penetrate through the finite to its infinite ground. Christian theology, in particular, will further interpret it as belonging to the created goodness of humanity.

Once we understand economic development or *freedoms* as embedded in, empowered by, and released by excellence as *clearing* (opening), the task of inducing and sustaining economic growth and development becomes the task of creating and maintaining a healthy vibrant *clearing*. Development is no longer only about quantitative increases in national output or acquisition of capabilities for freedom as it moves beyond *development as freedom* to fundamentally *development as excellence.*

This *excellentist* philosophy is the ideational framework of economic development that leads us beyond economic development itself. Development as freedom is a particular perspective that reveals merely the context of an opposition to the current paradigm of economic development but not the development of humanity itself. The holistic perspective is this: It is in knowing the human in her self-transcendence to grasp the be-ing in which freedoms proper to capability enhancement flow, and by that she comes to development and so comes to herself and there she goes beyond herself.

Her ability *to be* and seize her own possibilities is the primitive and primary freedom to participate in this process of self-enactment that is economic development. She acts economically or developmentally as she has being (ability to be) and is in her being. Economic development is one of the freedoms to participate fully in the process of transcendence, and it is itself embedded in this process.

Development as excellence asks not about a particular paradigm of economic development but about human development as such, about the human nature, the human impulse toward the future, and human self-transcendence, which are presupposed in any encounter with economic reality. It is also about the philosophical-theological character of every economic action that is in it insofar as it is. Economic development is a category of human excellence and has its basis in it. Economic growth or development presupposes a human subject and an object (for example, human flourishing) about which it is directed that in turn presupposes beings actualizing their potentialities. The philosophy of excellence is the system of ideas in terms of which every form of economic achievement can be interpreted and which expresses ultimately the general principles that are requisite to the ethical analysis of any paradigm of economic development whatsoever.

Excellence is the depth of economic development and is manifest through it – and both point to the ground of existence. Economic development keeps endlessly transcending the finite realities of forms of economic organization, production and distribution, and freedoms, yet remains bound to excellence, which bears it along. In this way of putting the matter, the theological character of every form, phase, and era of economic development is easy to discern. The power of transcendence points to a subject (man, woman) whose mind is directed to experience its own unlimited potentialities and who belongs to that which lies beyond the *margin* of the achieved and not-yet achieved, beyond nothing, beyond non-being—to being-itself. As Paul Tillich puts it:

The fact that man never is satisfied with any stage of his finite development, the fact that nothing finite can hold him, although finitude is his destiny, indicates the indissoluble relation of everything finite to being-itself. Being-itself is not infinity; it is that which lies beyond the polarity of finitude and infinite self-transcendence. Being-itself manifests itself to finite being in the infinite drive of the finite beyond itself.[18]

In the light of these points, the ethical framework developed in this essay becomes the basis not only of ideas for forging a suitable social ethics of excellence, but also of ideas that speak directly to the design and dynamics of economic development – and indeed the philosophy of economic development.

Excellence as the Next Small Thing

Excellence is not a call for perfection that paralyzes actions or morality, but a call for doing the next small thing. It is about going the extra mile, about saying, "I cannot continue but I must." It is about making things better one at time, making the small changes that will add up to a revolution. If one wants to go from A to D, excellence is not about taking a giant leap from A to D, but going from A to B, to C, and ultimately to D consistently. The developed countries are not the way they are today because they built everything at once. It is here a little, there a little. It is all about making every small change, every small decision, every small repair, every small invention, and every small project count for something. Let the next small thing you do as a leader count, and herein lies the power of the marginalist thinking that has revolutionized modern economics.

Let us attempt to learn to reap the benefit of the marginalist thinking that created neoclassical economics. Managerial economics is about making good decisions at the margin on a daily basis. We may not always like neoclassical economics as it sometimes works against the common good or the masses, but we can learn something from it about the power of the margin that sustains excellence.

For economists, excellence (or what in very technical terms is called optimality) is at the margin. "Operate at the margin" is their mantra for excellence. In order to maximize profit, a firm is to operate at the level of production where *marginal cost* equals the *marginal revenue.* In simple terms, this means the cost of producing one item, the marginal item, should balance the revenue from selling it. The return from the employment of labour is maximized when the marginal productivity of labour (the additional output as a result of adding one more worker) equals the marginal wage for the incremental worker. Deciding the excellent way to allocate a society's capital, for instance, depends on figuring out the *next best alternative* use to which the capital currently employed in one area should be redeployed. This is to say, the value to society of any particular asset is assessed by whether or not it is earning the *marginal rate of return* currently obtainable. The resources of an economy are excellently allocated when it operates on its *production possibility frontier,* the line of marginality between what is attainable and what is not yet attainable.

On a lighter note, let me end this discourse about the economic concept of excellence with a short story. An economist friend once told me that Ezekiel's God is a marginalist, a Deity concerned with the *next small thing*. He said that Ezekiel's God (chapter 33:12–20) stated that a person is punished and condemned for his or her marginal (incremental) act of sin even if he or she has always lived without disobedience. Similarly, a sinner is saved by his next act of obedience. God declared this approach to deciding whom to reward with life and whom to make suffer death, which is all based on repentance or act of sin at the margin, as just and fair. So my economist-interlocutor concluded that Ezekiel's excellent God is concerned with acts done at the *margin*.

The point to take home here is that excellence is not an ideal of perfection that finds us inadequate and dehumanized and wishing to depart from all the necessity of the human (Nigerian) context. But it is an opening, a clearing in the great current of life that affirms our characteristically human way of being. It is a clearing beyond perfection that allows us to explore the manifestation of our hidden potentialities, which affirms and fulfils our humanity.

Excellence as presented in this essay is not posited to give "the image of an anthropomorphic perfection" obtained by the removal of all constraints that the best of human life depends on.[19] The striving for realization of potentialities is not merely about escaping problems and human limits (in the vulgar sense that Martha Nussbaum condemns), but principally about expanding and extending what is natural and normal for human beings to do. In the pursuit of excellence the person does not transcend what is morally obligatory good for him or her to do. It is about creating possibilities (as one strives to realize one's potentialities) that transcend what is now given, what is now ordinary (in the multiple terms of morality, technological, politics, economics, arts, etc.) in a direction that is positive to communality, participation, and orientation to the infinite.

Summary and Conclusion

Excellence, in a certain fundamental sense, "is" the infinite longing of humans to actualize their potentialities, to reach the new, and to reveal the future. The process of revelation for communities needs an authentic leader. Such a leader and his or her followers not only invent and proclaim the new, but they are absolutely seized by what is happening and are transfigured by it and are committed to building (or rebuilding) society piece by piece even from a place of nothingness. The authentic leader tells his or her people that they have built into them the strivings for excellence to continually surpass themselves and the very contours of any particular existence. He or she places a demand on them to actualize their potentialities. This is the new kind of leadership that a moral vision of excellence demands.

Alas, there is another demand on every African. A demand necessitated by the emerging global civilization, the poverty and humiliation of Africans, and the circumstantially contingent ground-level placement of blackness among the human race. The civilizing, globalizing process unfolding itself before us raises questions about blackness, placing a demand on all Africans. The demand that confronts us is the urgent need to express our excellence, to fulfil that which is not alien to our nature. The demand for excellence is our own essence and it is grounded in blackness. Today's actuality of blackness is not the true complete blackness, not the fulfilment of what is intended for black people. At best, it is a forward reference to fulfilment, an ignored prompting to perform the musical score that has never been performed. The fulfilment of blackness involves confronting and affirming the demand as an *ought*. We experience this demand not only for ourselves but also in our encounter with other races and colours. The content of the demand is that Africans be accorded the same dignity as others. This is the dignity of lifting humanity to its intended fulfilment, being a sturdy bearer of excellence, being free from crushing poverty and dilapidating diseases.

REFERENCES

[i] For quotes, see Jean-Luc Nancy's work in Jean-Luc Nancy, *The Inoperative Community*, translated by Peter Connor, Lisa Garbus, Michael Holland, and Simona Sawhney, with foreword by Christopher Fynsk. (Minneapolis: University of Minnesota Press, 1991), x, xxxvii.

[ii] There is no time or space to go into detailed philosophical analysis here. I refer the curious reader to my book, *The Principle of Excellence: A Framework for Social Ethics* (Lanham, Maryland: Lexington Books, 2009).

[iii] Aristotle *Nicomachean Ethics*, Book One, 7, 1097a 19.

[iv] The word is used in the old philosophical sense and not in the common, vulgar sense of the erotic. By *eros* I mean, "the force which holds the world together and keeps it alive, anthropologically and cosmologically; the power of attraction which unites, and the individual weight which simultaneously distinguishes. The rhythm of attraction and distance, affection and respect is the power of *eros*." See Jürgen Moltmann, *The Spirit of Life: A Universal Affirmation* (Minneapolis: Fortress Press, 1992), 196.

[v] Mihaly Csikszentmihalyi, *Flow: The Psychology of Optimal Experience* (New York: HarperCollins Publishers, 1990), 72-73.

[vi] Roberts Merrihew Adams, *A Theory of Virtue: Excellence in Being for the Good* (Oxford: Oxford University Press, 2006), 89-91 for an argument about how

concern for the good of persons is linked with caring for some activities for their own sake.

8. I have borrowed the rhetorical flourish of Oscar Cullman in a different context for my purpose here. Oscar Cullman, Harry A. Wolfson, Werner Jaeger, and Henry J. Cadbury, *Immortality and Resurrection: Death in the Western World: Two Conflicting Currents of Thought* (New York: The Macmillan Company, 1965), 19.

[viii] Amartya Sen, *Development as Freedom* (New York: Random House, 1999).

[ix] Victor Zuckerkandl, *Sound and Symbol: Music and the External World* (London: Routledge and Kegan Paul, 1956), 252.

[x] Zuckerkandl, *Sound and Symbol*, 252.

[xi] Zuckerkandl, *Sound and Symbol*, 253.

[xii] Zuckerkandl, *Sound and Symbol*, 252.

[xiii] Zuckerkandl, *Sound and Symbol*, 12.

[xiv] Zuckerkandl, *Sound and Symbol*, 15.

[xv] For the generation of melody and rhythms, this is what Zuckerkandl (*Sound and Symbol*, 248) says:

A tone sounding on uninterruptedly is not yet melody and not yet rhythm. Strictly speaking, melody begins not with the first tone but with the first step from tone to tone. In the same way, rhythm is not born with the first sounding of a tone but with the first interruption and the sounding of a new tone (or the new sounding of the same tone).

[xvi] Here I am writing under the inspiration of Zuckerkandl's analysis of tones. See his *Sound and Symbol*, 20.

[xvii] This is a reversal of Paul Tillich's thought in *Systematic Theology: Existence and the Christ, vol. 2* (Chicago: University of Chicago Press, 1957), 25.

xviii Tillich, *Systematic Theology: Reason and Revelation, Being and God*, vol. 1 (Chicago: University of Chicago Press, 1951), 191.

xiv Martha C. Nussbaum, *Love's Knowledge: Essays on Philosophy and Literature* (New York: Oxford University Press, 1990), 371.

Chapter Five
WHO SHOULD HAVE OWNERSHIP RIGHT TO NATURAL RESOURCES?
John Boye Ejobowah

Who ought to have rights to natural resources? Is it the state or the landowner under whose land the resources are located? Not much has been done to answer this question. The great classical liberal philosophers did not give much attention to this issue, the exception being the late Victorian utilitarian, Henry Sidgwick. Contemporary philosophers have not addressed the question head on either; instead they mention the issue in passing while discussing territorial rights. For example, the late John Rawls, unarguably the most influential twentieth-century liberal philosopher, did not discuss it. He made only an oblique reference to natural resources belonging to the people while discussing the role of "a people's government" in maintaining "their territory" (Rawls 1999: 38).

Perhaps the exceptions to the contemporary philosophers are the cosmopolitans who maintain that individuals everywhere are moral equals, that territorial boundaries are contingencies which are morally arbitrary, and that, as moral equals, individuals have rights to natural resources of the earth. Thomas Pogge (1994) is most representative of the cosmopolitans. He begins with the supposition that all the resources of the earth belong to everyone, a supposition that is standard in the natural rights theory. He ends up with the notion that nation states can use resources within their jurisdictions but have to pay a consumption tax – a global resource tax – which will be used to alleviate global poverty. His logic is that natural resources belong to everyone by nature, and if a group of persons draw political boundaries around a swath of land on the face of the earth and the resources therein, the rest of the global poor have to be paid taxes for the resources that are enclosed and being used up. Pogge's position is not one that I wish to take. It is incoherent to claim that a state has right to resources within its territory but has to pay for exercising that right. Such a claim amounts to subordinating sovereign right to global humanity (Miller 2010: 4).

How then, should one go about answering the above question? Perhaps the best way is to begin with Locke's idea of property acquisition. Locke provides a template for understanding ways in which property is acquired and ways that an individual's right to property in land gets translated into state jurisdictional right over a territory. Although Locke's ideas about the transition from individual ownership of land (in the state of nature) to state jurisdictional right over a territory have been challenged by contemporary writers including Brilmayer (1989) and Stilz (2009), they nonetheless provide important roadmaps to answering the question of who ought to own rich natural resources. One such important roadmap is that in the transition from the state of nature to civil society, individuals do not give up their property rights in land to the state, and that the latter acquires jurisdictional rights to a territory following the contract. One of the initial claims this paper makes is that the state has jurisdictional right, not property right, to a territory, and that Lockean principles would disqualify the state from having incidental rights to natural resources within the territory in so far as the latter is not its property.

Lockean principles about property acquisition also lead to another initial claim: it is the claim that natural resources are not the product of the landowner's labour and that the boundaries of surface landholdings do not have meaning at the subsurface levels. On these bases, the paper notes that assigning ownership to the landowner would not be justified.

Having made these initial claims, I create tension in my argument by noting that there are other principled grounds on which the state and the landowner could justifiably make claims to natural resources. Some of these principles are fully Lockean. For example, in the case of the state, Locke notes that it becomes a landowner after society has been formed. Its lands are public lands, lands that belonged to no one and were hemmed in when individuals brought their respective lands under political rule. In such lands, it would be reasonable for the state to make claim to natural resources, so I argue. Then there is the power of the state to take what belongs to others when it is in an emergency situation and if such taking would keep it alive. This power of eminent domain is not Lockean, but it finds support in all the great natural law theorists, including Grotius and Puffendorf. In the case of the individual landowner, I note that Lockean principles of property acquisition would defend her claim on two grounds: if she appropriates resources directly under her land and if she controls access points to resources underground.

Once the merits and demerits of the opposing parties' positions have been laid out as indicated above, the next inevitable step is to work out the requirements of justice. Here I consider a range of possible alternative judgments and settle for one that reflects the interest of the parties concerned. The main point the paper attempts to establish is this: the determination of natural resource ownership has to reflect the interest of the landowner and of the state that has political jurisdiction of the territory, and simultaneously reward the entrepreneur who takes the risk of discovering and appropriating the resources. Before launching into this argument, I explain in the next section below two accounts of resource rights and why these accounts are not satisfying. The two accounts are Sidgwick's utilitarian view and a statist conception that regards the territory and resources within it as state property.

Two Accounts of Resource Rights

Henry Sidgwick was one of the few classical liberals that paid attention to natural resource rights. Like most classical liberals before him, Sidgwick regarded the application of labour to the commons as the source of ownership right. With respect to mineral resources below the surface of the soil, his view was that they are not related to the labour or care of the surface landowner and that the government or individual members of the political community should have rights to them.

His argument was not that simple. He reflected over the idea of depriving the surface landowner of the right to resources while permitting other members of the community to enjoy the right. He addressed this issue by using his utilitarian principle. As a utilitarian moral theorist, Sidgwick proclaimed that "the true standard and criterion by which right legislation is to be distinguished from wrong is conduciveness to the ... happiness of the individual human beings who compose the community" (*Ibid,* 34). Using this principle as a guide, Sidgwick tried to determine the option that would generate the most happiness. His answer was that the surface owner may be the last person to know about the existence of extractable and economically valuable mineral resources below the surface. Therefore, there will be no utility whatsoever if the right is associated with surface landownership. In light of this consideration, Sidgwick determined that it is "best to retain for the government, or allow to individual members of the community generally, the right of extracting minerals from lands owned by others." However, this will be subject to the condition that adequate compensation be paid to the owner of the surface land and that extraction should be avoided in parts of the land where the activity will cause inconvenience to the surface owner (Sidgwick 1891: 73). This option facilitates the promotion of the happiness of the community (including the surface owner). So, Sidgwick's utilitarianism, like any other utilitarian moral theory, is consequentialist. A theory is consequentialist if it uses a good outcome as the standard for judging a moral action. Utilitarianism is consequentialist because for it, the morality of an act depends solely on the promotion of happiness or pleasure.

The seeming merit in Sidgwick's consequentialist moral argument is that the interest of the surface landowner is not discounted completely. Utilitarianism is often criticized for its ruthless exploitation of the interests of the minority in order to achieve "a net gain of total utility" (Brown 2004: 14). By prescribing compensation payment, Sidgwick seems to counter this charge, but he does not succeed in doing so. His two major claims effectively rule out the surface owner as having rights to mineral resources. The two claims, to repeat, are that subsurface mineral resources are not related to the labour of the surface owner and that the latter may not promote utility as he or she may not have knowledge of the existence of underground rich resources. These claims do not invite compensatory payment. Conceptually, compensation is reparation for damages due to a wronged individual. In Sidgwick's utilitarian thought, compensation arises when a person causes "mischief" or "injury" to others without having taken proper steps to prevent such injury or mischief in the first place (Sidgwick 1891: 111). And compensation is mainly, but not exclusively, for material damages or injuries to reputation (*Ibid,* 115-117). Going by this idea, the exploitation of mineral resources by persons other than the landowner does not amount to mischief or material damage, for the landowner does not have rights to rich resources below the surface. Material damage arises if there is environmental degradation or the land is taken away. Where there is no such degradation or loss of land, the surface owner may not have a legitimate basis for compensation claims. In effect, Sidgwick's argument does not recognize the landowner has having claims to rich resources below the surface of her estate.

Further, Sidgwick's idea that government or individuals should have the right to extract minerals is somewhat vague. It is whether it is the government that has the right to resources or whether it is individuals (not necessarily the surface landowner). If it is the government, that would eliminate individuals, and if it is the latter, that would also take out the former. So his use of the "or" is somewhat confusing. Yet it should not be confusing. Since the overall aim of Sidgwickian legislation is to increase general happiness, minerals resources have to be up for anyone with either the scientific knowledge to accord them economic importance or the appropriate technology to discover and extract them from under the soil. Anyone with these abilities will contribute immensely to the economic growth and development of society and, in this way, maximize happiness. From this standpoint, either individuals or government have to exercise rights to mineral resources if either of them discover such resources under lands owned by others. The implication of this utilitarian consequentialist thought is obvious: the landowners have to lose out.

In contrast, there is the view that regards natural resources as belonging to the sovereign (McCorquodale, 2001). For some, the sovereign is the state and the state owns what is in its territory. McCorquodale (2001: 146) conveys this impression when he writes that "all natural resources, whether located under the soil or under the sea … are deemed to be in the control of the owner of the territory, that is, the state." The view here is that the territory is a property of the state, and natural resources therein belong to the latter. This view of sovereignty is unsatisfying for three reasons. First, the state is disconnected from the people and emerges as a proprietor that "owns" everything, including the people, within its territorial boundaries (*Ibid*, 142). This view of sovereignty enables rulers to abrogate to themselves the right to sell off resources within their territories for private benefit. This was certainly the case in several resource-rich developing countries during the Cold War era when authoritarian rulers maintained coercive control over their respective national populations (Wenar 2008: 12-13). Second and related to the above, it has the danger of justifying state appropriation of a people's rich natural resources. Where a new sovereign state is established (by any means, including occupation of unclaimed territory, accretion, etc.) and the territorial boundaries of the new state are drawn to include an unwilling group (and, as a consequence, its territory), the unwilling group will forfeit its resources to the new state. Finally, the idea can be used by a powerful ruler or a group of persons that control a state to annex territories on the other side of its borders with a view to seizing rich natural resources therein (Moore 1998). Saddam Hussein's 1990 invasion and occupation of Kuwait is a prime example.

For others, the sovereign is the people and the state is their creation (Wenar 2008; Nine 2010). In this case the primary possessor of rights to territory and to resources within the territory is the people. Cara Nine (2010: 17) expresses this view when she argues that "a collective that settles in a geographical region acquires resource rights within that region as it demonstrates its capacity to establish justice through the rule of law over those particular resources." Also, she notes that it is the collective (the people) who can "establish legitimate rule of law within a region" and it is this collective – not individuals – that has the right to resources (*Ibid*, 19). This view that regards the people as having rights to resources is Lockean inspired. In Locke's theory, the people are sovereign and they authorise an ensemble of institutions (the state) to act on their behalf. In his theory, the state is an institutional agent of the people, and following Locke's ideas, I henceforth use the word state in the collective sense (people) and for the sake of convenience I also use it interchangeably with the word the people.

Yet I do not endorse Nine's Lockean-inspired view, because it does not account for a theoretical shift from individual rights to collective rights. In Lockean classical liberalism, individuals are the rights holders, and it is these individuals that assemble to constitute first a society and then a government. The above view that regards resources as belonging to the people does not tell how individual rights to property change to collective rights. Cara Nine (2010: 11) acknowledges that "Lockean principles ... specifically ... establish individual rights to property," yet there is no statement within the four walls of her article that accounts for the leap from individual to collective rights. Admittedly, in liberalism a people's jurisdictional rights over a territory carry the power to make laws within that territorial space as Nine rightly argues, but this power to make laws does not translate into property rights. I accept that the power to make laws belongs to the people (the sovereign), but this is distinct from property rights for which the holder is the individual. The view that regards the people as the owner of resources does not account for ways in which rights that are anchored on the individual becomes collective rights. Also, it does not explain why the original rights holder, the individual, would no longer matter. In what follows below, I give an account of an inclusive right to natural resources.

Inclusive Rights to Natural Resources

The Lockean theory of rights contains the following arguments. First, individuals have natural rights and liberty prior to society and also have equal access to the gifts of nature. Second, individuals acquire the right to property by applying their labour to the gifts of nature. For example, by enclosing or tilling an unoccupied land, an individual acquires right to that very land. Third, there is no standard law and no government in the state of nature, and as such rights are not secured; instead of property, individuals have possessions. When these three propositions are added together, we find that in Lockean theory, "the great and chief end" of individuals constituting a society and government is the "preservation of their property" (Locke 1980 §124).

If property rights, especially right to land, are held by individuals, can the people – the sovereign – also become a holder of such rights? In the Lockean view, individuals uniting in a society also annex and "submit to the community" those possessions which they have acquired or shall acquire and are not under any government (Locke 1980 § 120). Yet the people – or their institutional representative, the state – does not become property owner by this account. In the process of uniting in a society, individuals subject their lands to the laws of the sovereign. The sovereign exercises jurisdictional rights, not property rights. Jurisdictional rights are powers to make laws – laws that regulate persons and property rights within a given territory (Meisels 2005: 7-8). Call it territorial powers. It is on the basis of these laws that natural rights become civil rights. It is impossible to speak of civil property rights where there is no jurisdictional authority. Civil rights impose correlative duty on others to observe the rights in question, and it is the political authority, through its laws backed by coercive power, that ensures that the correlative duty is performed. For example, if X has rights to a piece of land L, others have a duty not to take or occupy L. The duty that others owe X is to do nothing (don't touch L), and the performance of this duty is ensured by the system of justice supported by a threat to use the monopoly of force (see Ostrom and Schlager 1996: 130). In this respect, jurisdictional authority is necessary for civil rights. Without the former there can be no justice or injustice, and individuals would have might not right, as Hobbes (1968: 202-203) famously noted. This is not to suggest that, in Lockean theory, a state exercising territorial right must first come into existence; instead while forming a society, individuals also give up their natural liberties. The contract simultaneously generates a civil society and a change from natural property rights to civil property rights.

Lea Brilmayer has raised questions about the contractarian origin of jurisdictional rights over a territory. According to her, individuals who participated in the contract had private property rights, not sovereign rights over a territory. In her view, it is a mystery that private individuals who had private property rights can grant territorial powers they did not possess (Brilmayer 1989: 15). Cara Nine has responded to Brilmayer's query by arguing that on Lockean principles of desert and efficiency, the collective (represented by the state) can come to have territorial rights to land. She notes, correctly, that labour is the source of value and ownership rights, but she goes on to say that the "state is a unique and significant author of the land's value in several ways," including making laws that make for stable system of agriculture, effecting economic and technological improvements, and making cultural investments that shape the appearance of the landscape (Nine 2008: 159-160). There are two problems with this response.

First, Nine presents the territory as a property of the people. In the Lockean theory of rights acquisition, the people do not apply their labour to the land and they are not property owners. It is individuals who own land by mixing their labour with it. The idea that the people have collectively applied their effort to a piece of land and therefore own that "particular piece of land" is foreign to Lockean principles (*Ibid*, 160). Second, Nine does not really respond to Brilmayer's query, as she assumes the existence of the people prior to the formation of civil society. The idea that the people invested their labour in the land assumes that individuals were united in the pre-political state and that the people enter society as the holders of rights to a particular land. A persuasive response to Brilmayer has to explain how the individual right to land holdings translates into collective a territorial right.

A discussion of the ways that the rights of individuals to their respective land holdings translate into state territorial right is beyond the scope of this paper. It will suffice to say that, conceptually, a territory is a combination of land, the population living on the land, and the political institutions that govern the population on the land (Miller 2010). It describes a physical space within which political jurisdiction is exercised, different from mere land that is simply real estate. Following Gottmann (1975: 29), I define territory to mean the "physical container and support of the body politic organized under a governmental structure." In my view, territory in Lockean theory springs from consent to form a political society. Consent to form a political society includes consent to submit one's land to the community's authority. In Locke's words, "it would be a direct contradiction for anyone to enter into society with others for the securing and regulating of property and yet to suppose his land, whose property is to be regulated by the laws of society, should be exempt from the jurisdiction of that government ..." (Locke 1980 § 120). The very acts by which individuals establish a society and government are the very acts by which they turn over their natural rights (to protect their respective lands) to the people's authority. Thus, the people exercise jurisdictional rights over the aggregated lands and over individual members. While individual members of the body politic have ownership right to their respective lands, the state has jurisdiction over the physical space defined by the totality of individual members' lands. Having jurisdictional rights means having the right to legislate and execute laws within a definite territorial space, impose taxes for good government, and mount defence against external invaders. On this score, the territory is not a property but a jurisdictional domain of the people. An extensive version of the Lockean argument that grounds territorial jurisdiction on individual landownership right has been made by Simmons (2001).

If the territory is not a property of the state, could the later claim the right to its natural resources? Logically, the absence of property ownership should not confer appurtenance rights. An appurtenance is a thing that is attached to a principal thing so that ownership of the latter confers incidental right to the former. For example, if I own a land and there is an orange tree on it, that tree is mine. My claim to the orange tree presupposes my ownership of the land. Similarly, for the state to claim appurtenance rights, it must first satisfy a condition – to own the territory as a property just as I own a piece of land. If this condition is satisfied, and resources are assumed to be attached to the territory, the state can justifiably claim rights. However, the state has a jurisdictional right which is different from property rights. The former is not reducible to the later and should not serve as a basis for claiming incidental rights, contrary to arguments by Cara Nine.

Further, the Lockean principle of right acquisition would hardly defend the collective's claim to natural resources. By definition, natural resources are raw materials that are not made by humans. They exist by nature; it is the extraction that requires human labour. The state cannot plausibly own resources if it has not worked its labour on them.

Some may claim that the state could have ownership by virtue of its right of eminent domain. The right of eminent domain is the power of the state to take any property within the territory for its use. For example, the state could pull down an entire block of private buildings because it needs the land to build a railroad or public utilities. Natural law theorists such as Hugo Grotius, Samuel von Pufendorf, Corlenius van Bynkershoek, and Emerich de Vattel wrote about this power of "takings" but conditioned it on public necessity and compensation payments. By the Lockean theory of consent, it is a puzzle why the people would acquire the right to take citizens' property. Individuals in the state of nature did not possess the right to take each other's property and could not have transferred to the state what they did not have: the right of takings. So, why would the state have this power to confiscate? There is a philosophical difficulty in individuals granting more powers than they originally possessed (Paul 2008: 77). Following Sandefur (2003: 584), the power of takings could be considered a necessity, an emergency situation that justifies infringement on property rights. In the words of Grotius:

> A right, even when it has been acquired by subjects, may be taken away by the King in two modes: either as a Penalty, or by the force of Eminent Dominion. *But to do this by the force of Eminent Dominion, there is required, in the first*

> *place, public utility; and next, that, if possible,*
> *compensation be made, to him who has lost what*
> *was his, at the common expense* (Grotius 1853: Bk.
> II chap. XIV § 7. Emphasis not in original.)

Grotius' discussion of the right of a starving person to the excesses of another underlies the idea that an individual in an emergency situation could violate right in order to save her own life. To illustrate, a farmer who gets lost in the forest for several days and is starving to near death suddenly comes across a cabin likely stocked with food. The lost and starving farmer would do what is reasonably required for her to survive – break into the cabin and eat what she can. If there is a box of jewellery in the cabin, it would not be reasonable for the starving farmer to help herself to that. The act of breaking into the cabin to get food is not classic theft; it is an infringement of right, but necessity will excuse the infringement. From the standpoint of Grotius, the infringement is a debt the farmer has to repay. Just as in the case of individuals, necessity may make the state take the unavoidably reasonable step of taking private property in order to preserve itself. However, compensation has to be paid, and in doing so rights are respected. The right of eminent domain, therefore, assumes respect for property rights. It does not presuppose arbitrary power of the state to take whatever is in the territory and without compensation. On this ground, the state ought not to use the power of eminent domain to take natural resources it does not own and if such taking is not justified by necessity.

Does the above argument open the door for the landowner to have ownership rights? I don't think so. It is difficult to view the landowner as having ownership rights, and for good reasons. First, going by Locke's argument that grounds property rights on the application of labour to the gifts of nature, it will be inconceivable to think of the landowner as having mixed her labour with mineral deposits that, in some cases, could be more than a kilometre below her surface soil and which she has never seen or touched. While it is meaningful to claim a right to structures and plants on the land, it is illogical to claim that an individual has applied her labour to minerals deep underground because that individual owns the surface soil. It is equally problematic to make such a claim on the grounds that ownership of the surface includes ownership of the subsurface deep down, for the depth of the soil that is associated with the surface land is limited. If the depth that is associated with the surface were to be without limit, then it would extend all the way to the core of the earth. But that is not the case because the land area gets narrower as one digs deeper below. Hence, for example, an expanse of land that is 500,000 acres on the surface will not be more than a fraction of a millimetre as one digs away from the earth crust toward the core. Also, the thickness of the solid earth (the earth crust) ranges from thirty kilometres (in most places) to fifty kilometres (under the mountains). Beyond this distance is magma to which no surface landowner can meaningfully make claim. The twelfth-century Latin maxim "*cujus est solum eius est usque ad coelum et usque ad inferos*" ("whoever owns the soil owns all the way to heaven and all the way to the depths") is just too sweeping (Jacobs 1998: xi). A maxim that attributes to the landowner the entire space from the core of the earth to the outer limits of the atmosphere is unscientific and impractical. Sidgwick was right when he noted that mineral resources are not the product of the surface owner's labour and are not related to her improvement of the land.

Second, mineral deposits may lie below lands owned by different persons, and no landowner can sensibly isolate and make claim to the section of resources under her surface land. For example, groundwater, oil, and gas are fluid and they stretch underground across surface land boundaries.

Where the surface land comprises numerous holdings, it will be unreasonable to say that each surface owner has rights to what is underneath her soil. Such a view would amount to saying that I have exclusive ownership rights to the section of the stream that runs through my land. Making a rights claim and drilling groundwater or oil under my land will drain the groundwater and oil underneath the adjourning land, thereby depriving the adjourning owner of rights. Also, being liquid, groundwater and oil that are under my land this year may migrate laterally to others' lands, with the result that if I had ownership, the substance to which I have ownership would be non-existent when I try to get hold of it. Owning a substance entails being able to take physical possession of it. Ownership is meaningless if the substance has a common supply source and has not been separated from the common source.

Third, with advances in modern science and technology, individuals can mix their labour with resources deep underground without having to operate directly from the overhead surface land. For example, it is possible to find and to slant drill oil from a distant and unrelated surface location. Slant drilling is the act of drilling non-vertical oil wells to reach deposits without having to operate directly from or trespass onto the surface land above the reservoir. In this case, it may not be reasonable to deny rights to the individual who applied her labour to and took possession of the subsoil oil from a distant surface land. In any case, it will be hard to determine with certainty the particular subsoil from which the oil was derived. It would be difficult to prove that the oil was pumped from under X's land or form under Z's land. Given all these considerations, it will not be defensible to vest the landowner with rights to natural resources.

However, there are grounds on which both the landowner and the state could have rights. The landowner could make a valid claim by operating from her soil to extract migratory mineral resources under the surface. She owns the resources once she gets hold of and has absolute possession of them, even though the resources may have migrated to the point of operation where they were extracted. This is called the rule of capture; under this rule, the landowner does not own migratory natural resources under her estate but has absolute rights the moment she appropriates them (Kuntz 1957: 406). For example, if I dig a well in my backyard the water that percolates into the well is my property. Before it percolated, the water was unappropriated and belonged to everyone. Similarly, prior to appropriation, mineral resources are subject to extraction from a common source by anyone acting from within the boundaries of her property. In extracting from the common source, the landowner must dig vertically downward and any groundwater, oil, or gas that enters the casing of the well is her rightful property. In this respect, the landowner could legitimately have ownership rights by operating within the confinement of her land. However, if the well slants and bottoms under another person's land, trespass would have been committed (Kuntz 1957). This argument is valid to the extent that the landowner is the one that discovers the mineral resources and actually digs the well. In reality, this is not the case. Very often it is the risk taker, the entrepreneur, who invests in mineral exploration and exploitation. Her labour has to be taken into account while determining the rights of the landowner.

Furthermore, the landowner could reasonably claim rights if the resources do not migrate away and are close to her land surface. Some minerals, especially solid ones, are a few centimetres away from the earth's surface and do not escape from one land boundary to another. Such minerals cannot be extracted without operating on the very surface land under which they are located. Since the land is controlled by the owner, access to the minerals is automatically controlled by the owner as well, and no one can reach the bounty without seeking her consent. By virtue of being the only one that has access to the land, the landowner has *de facto* possession of nature's bounties when they are discovered. It is rather like having undiscovered gold in the soil beneath the floor of my house; I effectively become the possessor when it becomes known that there is gold under the floor of my house. The landowner's situation satisfies one of Hume's main principles for property ownership, namely, constant or stable possession (Hume 194: 70-71). Bradbrook (1988: 464) made the point when he noted that solid minerals close to the surface "may be said to be effectively, if not legally, in the ownership of the surface landowner."

There are plausible grounds for the state to also make ownership claim. Although, Lockean principles sanction individual property rights, they also make room for "joint property" (Locke 1980: §35). Joint property refers to public lands. These are unappropriated lands surrounded by the lands of those who came together to form a political society. These lands were unappropriated when the society was created; they were ringed in when individuals freely consented to subject their lands to political authority. They are public lands "left common by compact" and "no one can inclose or appropriate any part, without the consent of his fellow commoners" (Locke 1980: §35). The state has a legitimate claim to natural resources on these lands that are common by compact, including resources on the continental shelf.

Also, to effectively perform the functions for which it was established, the state requires financial resources, resources that have to be transferred from private hands to public use (Epstein 1985: 4). The transfer could be done by voluntary donation, but voluntary donation is not a stable and sufficient revenue source. To ensure stable revenue, the state could lay claim to valuable natural resources that have not been appropriated by anyone. If the resources are under private lands and necessity requires that the state should take over these lands, it has to do so for "no state could survive" without the power of eminent domain (Puffendorf quoted in Paul 2008: 76). In this case, compensation has to be paid to the landowner.

If so, who should have rights? In short, what does justice require? Given that the state is a landowner (it owns public lands and the continental shelf), a possible solution is to recognize the landowners as having rights to mineral resources at the time of discovery. This would mean that the landowner – whether an individual or the state – would have absolute ownership rights the moment rich natural resources are discovered under the surface of her land. This solution is unsatisfactory for three reasons. First, it does not meet the earlier principle of property acquisition, namely, mixing labour with nature. Under this principle, the landowner has to apply her labour by capturing the resources under her land in order to be the owner. This is certainly not the case with this solution. Second, the solution does not account for the rights of the person who may have taken the risk of discovering the resources. Discovering mineral resources is an enterprise that requires labour, technical skills, and financial investment. It will be unjust to invest all the fruits of such an enterprise on the landowner and discount the adventurer whose enterprise yielded the discovery in the first place (Kuntz 1957). Third, it is unreasonable to give consideration to only the landowner, given that the subsurface soil does not belong to a particular landowner, that the surface land boundaries lose meaning as one digs downward away from the earth crust, and that minerals underground stretch horizontally and can hardly be tied with certainty to any surface landholding. In light of these considerations, it would not be fair to view the landowner as the sole owner of resources.

Another alternative is to consider both the landowner and the state as having rights, and the adventurer as deserving some claim to the fruit of her labour. Under this solution, every landowner whose surface land can serve as access point to minerals underground would have rights. Where operations are conducted on land X, but not on neighbouring land Y, the owner of neighbouring land Y would also have rights if access could have been be gained from land Y. The reasoning here is that by owning the surface land, the landowner automatically controls access to the resources below. And where there are small and numerous landholdings, it would not be feasible and efficient to mount operations on each plot of land, especially for minerals like oil and gas (the exception would be solid minerals that require open or strip mining). The state would equally have rights for some of the reasons given earlier – rich natural resources in the subsurface traverse several land boundaries; surface boundaries do not have meaning at the subsurface level; resources do not belong to anyone while they are in the subsurface unappropriated; and, driven by economic emergency, the state could invoke the power of eminent domain.

Conclusion

To conclude, I have used Lockean principles to present an inventory of the demerits and merits of the state's and landowner's claims to natural resources. I have also adjudicated the conflicting claims by considering the requirements of justice. I spelled out two possible solutions and determined that justice would require giving weight to the rights of the landowner and the state and also dignify the labour of the investor. With this conclusion, the landowner's rights are independent of compensation payments that follow land destruction. Indeed, compensation payments for ecological damage are additional to the landowners' share of rights. This conclusion is qualitatively different from Sidgwick's utilitarian position which sacrificed the right of the landowner at the altar of public good. While Sidgwick's consequentialist arguments prioritized the good over the right, this paper prioritized the right over the good.

References.

Bradbrook, Adrian. 1988. "The Relevance of the *Cujus est Solum* Doctrine to the Surface Landowner's Claim to Natural Resources Located above and Beneath the Land," *Adelaide Law Review*, 11: 262-483.

Brilmayer, Lea. 1989. "Consent, Contract and Territory," *Minnesota Law Review*, 74 (91): 1-35.

Brown, Peter G. 2004. "Are There Any Natural Resources?" *Politics and the Life Sciences*, 23 (1): 11-20.

Epstein, Richard A. *Takings: Private Property and the Power of Eminent Domain*, Cambridge, MA: Harvard University Press.

Gottmann, Jean. 1975. "The Evolution of the Concept of Territory," *Social Science Information*," 14 (3): 29-47.

Grotius, Hugo. 1853. *On the Rights of War and Peace (De Jure Velli et Pacis)*, edited by William Whewell, Cambridge: Cambridge University Press.

Hobbes, Thomas. 1968. *Leviathan*, with Introduction by C. B. Macpherson, London: Penguin.

Hume, David. 1948. A Treatise of Human Nature, Book III Part II, in *Hume's Moral and Political Philosophy*, edited with an introduction by Henry D. Aiken, New York: Hafner Press.

Jacobs, Harvey. 1998. Preface, in *Who Owns America? Social Conflict Over Property Rights*, edited by Harvey Jacobs, Madison: The University of Wisconsin Press.

Kuntz, Eugene. 1957. "The Law of Capture," *Oklahoma Law Review*, 10 (4): 406-409.

Locke, John 1980. *Second Treatise of Government*, edited with an introduction by C. B. Macpherson, Indianapolis, Indiana: Hackett Publishing

McCorquodale, Robert. 2001. International Law, Boundaries and Imagination, in *Boundaries and Justice: Diverse Ethical Perspectives*, edited by David Miller and Sohail H. Hashmi, Princeton, NJ: Princeton University Press.

Meisels, Tamar. (2009). *Territorial Rights*, Dordrecht, Netherlands: Springer.

Miller, David. 2010. "Jurisdictional Right: Concept and Justification," paper presented at the Ethnicity and Democratic workshop on Territory, Diversity and Citizenship, Donald Gordon Centre, Queen's University, Kingston Ontario, June 4-5.

Moore, Margaret. 1998. The Territorial Dimensions of Self-Determination, in *National Self-Determination and Secession*, edited by Margaret Moore, Oxford, UK: Oxford University Press.

Nine, Cara. 2010. "A Theory of Resource Rights: Resource Rights as Jurisdictional Authority," paper presented at the Ethnicity and Democratic workshop on Territory, Diversity and Citizenship, Donald Gordon Centre, Queen's University, Kingston Ontario, June 4-5.

Nine, Cara. 2008. "A Lockean Theory of Property," *Political Studies*, 56 (1): 148-165

Ostrom, Elinor and Edella Schlager. 1996. The Formation of Property Rights, in *Rights to Nature: Ecological, Economic, Cultural and Political Principles of Institutions for the Environment*, edited by Susan Hanna, Carl Folke, and Karl-Göran Mäler. Washington DC: Island Press.

Paul, Ellen Frankel. 2008. *Property Right and Eminent Domain*, New Brunswick, NJ: Transaction Publishers.

Pogge, Thomas. 1994. "An Egalitarian Law of Peoples," *Philosophy and Public Affairs*, 23 (3): 195-224.

Rawls, John. 1999. *The Law of Peoples*, Cambridge: Harvard University Press.

Sidgwick, Henry. 1891. *Elements of Politics*, London: Macmillan.

Simmons, A John. 2001. On the Territorial Rights of States, in *Social, Political, and Legal Philosophy: Philosophical Issues 11*, edited by Ernest Sosa and Enrique Villanueva, Malden, MA: Blackwell Publishers.

Stilz, Anna. 2009. "Why do States Have Territorial Rights," *International Theory*, 1 (2): 185-213.

Wenar, Lef. 2008. "Property Right and Resource Curse," *Philosophy and Public Affairs*, 36 (1): 2-30.

Wenar, Lef. 2005. "The Nature of Rights," *Philosophy and Public Affairs,* 33 (3):223-252.

Chapter Six
LEADERSHIP AND DEVELOPMENT CRISIS: THE OGONI EXPERIENCE
Nekabari Johnson Ntete-Nna

Introduction

The Ogoni are a minority ethnic group inhabiting an area of approximately 100,000 square kilometres east of Port Harcourt. The area forms part of the plains along the eastern fringes of the Niger Delta region. Traditionally, they are mainly farmers and fishermen. As ethnic minorities, they are relatively underdeveloped, in spite of the fact that the area produces petroleum, oil, and gas resources (the mainstay of the Nigerian economy). Writing on this paradox, Naanen (2003:69) maintains that:

> The Ogonis find themselves very much in this context of national poverty. However, consideration has to be given to the country's political peculiarities, which tend to be weighted heavily against minorities and indigenous groups. There is no statutory discrimination as the constitution recognises the equality of every citizen, but the dominant role of ethnicity and

other forms of prejudice in national affairs have placed ethnic minorities and indigenous groups at great disadvantage. Control or access to power in Nigeria and its state-centred economy can make a lot of difference between poverty and progress. Groups such as the Ogoni have largely remained marginal in the distribution of power, hence the entrenched discrimination they suffer. Such socio-economic inequality affects access to jobs, the provision of social facilities, the development of infrastructures and other economic opportunities. For instance, at the time of writing this report, around 50 per cent of Ogoni are still without electricity of the communities that have electricity, around 70 per cent of this only received it in 2000/2001.

This condition has turned for the worse. At the moment, no community in Ogoni has electricity or pipe-borne water, in spite of its proximity to the Afam power station, and primary health care facilities are in a deplorable state. As of the 2001-02 academic year, primary school enrolment stood at 178,649 while post-primary school enrolment in 2001 was 55,179. According to Naanen (2003), only 19.4 per cent of those who enrolled in primary schools were able to enter secondary schools in 1991, and in 2002, only 3,800 students or two per cent of the Ogoni population enrolled for various courses and programmes in tertiary institutions in Nigeria. The population of Ogoni was put at 837,239 in the 2006 Nigerian National Population Census. It was these issues which propelled Ogoni elites to form the Movement for the Survival of the Ogoni People (MOSOP) in 1990.

The organisation produced and published the Ogoni Bill of Rights in 1991. In the document, it demanded reparation for economic strangulation, environmental degradation, and political marginalisation by multinational oil companies and the Nigerian government, as well as the restructuring of the Nigerian federation to include political autonomy for minorities. The movement internationalised the struggle for ecological, economic, and political justice and for autonomy of the Ogoni people, when it gained membership of the Unrepresented Nations and Peoples Organisation in 1992 and began the process of networking with international environmental and human rights organisations, such as the Body Shop and Friends of the Earth, among others. The declaration by the United Nations General Assembly of the period 1993-2005 as the decade of the world's indigenous peoples provided the Ogoni with the opportunity to launch themselves into the international limelight and thus push their issues into global attention. Consequently, in January 1993, the Movement for the Survival of the Ogoni People (MOSOP) mobilised approximately 300,000 people in a non-violent protest march against the deplorable conditions of the Ogoni people.

Theoretical Framework

Many scholars, such as Saro-Wiwa (1994), Naanen (1995), and Nna (1999) have tried to locate the crisis of development in Ogoni within the context of the theory of internal colonialism. Wolpe (1975: 230) has identified two major characteristics of the internal colonialism model. They are:

1. The colonial relationship is conceived of as occurring between different countries, total populations, nations, and geographical areas or between peoples, different races, colours, and cultures.

2. The colonial relationship is characterised in a general way as involving domination, oppression, and exploitation.

According to McRoberts (1979: 294), the theory assumes that for various reasons (economic, political, and military) a stronger, more developed core region imposes itself upon a peripheral region, whose subsequent development is geared to the needs of the core. He explains that, "Out of this colonial relationship between regions, there develops a cultural division of labour in which high status positions are reserved for members of the core region and periphery population are relegated to lower positions".

Naanen (1995: 19) is a major exponent of this paradigm, with regard to the Ogoni question. According to him:

> Internal colonialism in Ogoniland is broadly characterised by certain fundamental developments. First, ethnic based political domination, which is used to expropriate Ogoni resources, especially oil and gas for the development of the power-controlling groups while the Ogoni remain underdeveloped and impoverished. Second, the alliance between these dominant groups – the multinational oil companies and state enterprises (which are controlled by the dominant group) operating in Ogoniland, which restricts the Ogoni's access to the modern and the more rewarding sectors of the Nigerian oil economy, establishing a pattern of economic discrimination against the Ogoni people. Third, oil-based environmental degradation, which gravely undermines the traditional peasants and fishing economy of the Ogoni leaving the people without a dependable alternative means of livelihood and fourth, gross and widespread human rights violation in Ogoniland.

Specifically, he maintains that:

> Ogoniland, which has produced more than
> 30 billion dollars worth of oil for Nigeria, has
> virtually nothing to show for this prodigious
> wealth. Ogoniland continues to exist in its original
> conditions; no potable water, no dependable
> health facilities, few useable roads, no electricity,
> no telecommunications and for the past three
> years, the schools have not been functioning
> because teachers have not been paid. Poverty and
> social deprivation are conspious. The mortality
> rate is high.

One element which is very consistent with the theory of internal colonialism but which is often ignored by scholars and analysts in the Ogoni situation is the issue of class. Indeed, in as much as the Ogoni are being exploited by outsiders, such exploitation is usually conducted through elements within the Ogoni society. The Ogoni elites for sure benefited from that relationship. The question that arises therefore is: to what extent does the Ogoni leadership share in the development or otherwise of their own community? What is the role of leadership in the process of development or underdevelopment of the Ogoni society?

Leadership

Leadership is often used within the context of the work environment, where it is conceived as the process of influencing employees to work towards the attainment of organisational goals or objectives (Lussien, 2002). Lemay (2002) defines it as the "exercise of authority in directing the work of others". As he puts it, "leadership may be formal or informal, when exercising authority, leadership. Leadership consists of getting people to do something the leader wants."

The concept of authority therefore is important in the conceptualisation of leadership. Leadership is consensual, and not imposed on the people. A ruler motivates his followers to attain the goals which they have set for themselves. As Sweeney and MacFarlin (2002) have observed, leadership is interpersonal influence aimed at motivating subordinates in creating a vision for the future and developing strategies for achieving goals. To Torrington and Chapman (1979), in exercising a dominant influence in an interpersonal group situation, a leader directs the behaviour of his subordinates towards the accomplishment of set goal.

Lemay (2002: 222) has identified twelve traits which have been accepted by scholars involved in leadership research as common to good leadership. They are: (1) achievement, (2) charisma, (3) creativity, (4) decisiveness (5) dependability, (7) enterprise, (8) intelligence, (8) judgement, (11) optimism (11) technical proficiency, and (12) verbal ability.

To Douglas McGregor, leadership is an interaction or a relationship built on four main variables. These are: (1) the character of the leader, (2) the followers' attitudes, needs, and other personal characteristics, (3) the organisation characteristics, such as its purpose structure and the nature of the tasks performed, and (4) the social, economic, and political milieu within which the organisation operates (cited in Lemay, 2002: 225).

Leadership, therefore, must have the capacity to envision, identify, and articulate the interests, wishes, aspirations, and goals of the society in which it operates. It must have the capacity to build consensus and mobilise, direct, and motivate the people towards the attainment of their set aspirations by mobilising the requisite human and material resources conducive to the growth and survival of the society.

Development

Development is a concept that is value-loaded. That perhaps explains why the definition varies. Jalloh (1989: 18) makes the point clear when he says:

> The meaning of the term development remains confusing and controversial in spite of or may be, because of the great deal of writing and discussion of which it has been the subject. It is doubtful that this lack of clarity and controversy can be resolved in the near future, for the meaning of a concept such as development is heavily laden with politics. This means that in the final analysis, the definition of the term is a function of one's position with respect to development, the interests and values that are likely to be affected by the realisation of development.

Seers (1995: 4) is emphatic that, "The starting point is that we cannot avoid what the positivists disparagingly refer to as value judgement. Development is inevitably a normative concept, almost a synonym for improvement. To pretend otherwise is just to hide our value judgement." He therefore conceives of development as the process of creating those conditions that are conducive for the realisation of the human personality. He stresses that, "its evaluation must therefore take into account three economic criteria: whether there has been a reduction in: (i) poverty, (ii) unemployment, (iii) inequality." (1995: 3)

The concern with development thus relates to how the human person is able to dominate his environment and thus actualise his dreams, goals, and aspirations. These issues are encapsulated in the concept of human development. According to the United Nations Development Programme (1995: 23), "Human development is a process of enlarging people's choices. In principle, these choices can be definite and change over time. But at all levels of development, the three essential ones are for people to live a long and healthy life, to acquire knowledge and to have access to resources for decent standard of living. If these essential choices are not available, many other opportunities remain inaccessible."

Interestingly, with regard to longevity, access to knowledge,, and decent living standards, the vast majority of Ogoni people are not developed. What accounts for this? Achebe (1983) provoked thought when he wrote that the problem with Nigeria is a problem with leadership. What is the problem with the leadership in Ogoni? Why has it not been able to act as catalyst for development?

The Role of Ogoni Leadership

The Ogoni lived in relative isolation from their neighbours long before contact with the British imperialists. Naanen (2003: 16) reveals that this relative isolation was the main reason why they escaped mention in the earlier European sources. He attributes this isolation to two main factors, namely (1) that the Ogoni refused to encourage intermarriage with any other groups apart from their Ibibio neighbours to the north-east as a way of sustaining their independence; and (2) that the Ogoni refused to participate in the transatlantic slave trade and hence escaped the attention of Europeans. He also reveals that they also refused to sign any treaty of protection with the British and resisted the imposition of British rule by force of arms. According to Naanen (2003: 17),

> Ogoni's fiercely independent disposition in historical times is abundantly attested to by the traditions of its neighbours and European records which also emphasise the people's reputation for hostility to outsiders. Other sources claimed

they were warlike and had a large reputation for cannibalism. These were important factors in explaining why Ogoni was never subjugated by any group as they successfully depended on their independence up to British conquest.

It was that conquest in 1914 through Major G.H. Walker which opened Ogoni to the outside world. Lacking in a common culture of elite recruitment, Ogoni depended on British modernisation efforts to raise its elites. The British introduced common law and established courts of law that resullted in the appointment of warrant chiefs, bailiffs, clerks and interpreters. Churches were opened, and so were schools and the Native Authority System. Fundamental to this process, however, was the introduction of representative democracy and thus competitive party politics towards the end of the colonial administration, resulting in the relative backwardness of Ogoni society compared to its neighbours with regard to development.

The first signs of organised leadership for the Ogoni people, therefore, came with the Ogoni Central Union in the 1940s. It was challenged by the backwardness of the Ogoni society which hampered its capacity to compete effectively with its rivals for positions in the emerging political order in Nigeria. It appealed to Ogoni sons and daughters to take the development of Ogoni as a challenge. In the preface to its Constitution, Rules, and Regulation, it declared:

> The Ogoni Central Union appeals to the youths and people in general wherever they are, reminding them of their backwardness and uneven position among other tribes of Nigeria and calling them to action. It appeals to those in authority: The Native Authority, the District Officer, the Resident and Chief Commission, Eastern Provinces for tolerance, sympathy and cooperation.

In the 1950s, the Union propelled the establishment of development infrastructures in Ogoni, including primary and secondary schools and dispensaries and the award of scholarship to indigent students of Ogoni extraction. However, the civil war and the opportunities provided by the emerging political order led to divisions among the rank of Ogoni elites. Writing on the situation in Biafra, Saro-Wiwa (1995: 51) observes:

The mentality of the educated Ogoni was always to keep close to the government of the day in order to pick up crumbs from the masters' table. Accordingly, although Ojukwu's rebel Biafran Government was hostile to the Ogoni as a people, the educated few were picking by grovelling at the feet of the administration.

The struggle for political appointment as a strategy for having access to the government and thus personal aggrandisement is fundamental to the Ogoni elite. It is also a veritable tool for dividing them. As Osaghe (1995) has observed:

The Ogoni have fared better than most other minorities (including oil producing minorities) in appointment to top government position, which is usually the yardstick for measuring access to state power... since the creation of Rivers State in 1967, every clan in Ogoni has provided one Minister or more at the federal and state levels in addition to other top political appointment.

It may be exaggerating to say that every clan in Ogoni has no access to such positions. It is, however, important to say that the quest for political appointment is important to the Ogoni elite. How that translates to the development of the Ogoni society is another issue altogether. The floodgates were opened with the creation of Rivers State in 1967. With the new state came opportunities for appointment into the executive council, boards of parastatals, etc., and thus, opportunities for primitive accumulation of wealth. In an attempt to protect their interest as a class, the elites formed the KAGOTE, an acronym for Khana, Gokana, Tai, and Eleme, the four clans in Ogoniland.

The principal members of the organisation were those who had served as pioneer members of the executive council of the new Rivers State. It has these same people who used their positions in government to carve out chieftaincy stools in Ogoni, making it the nationality with the highest number of first-class stools in the state (six in all). They mobilised the support of their patrons to appoint occupants of these positions either for themselves or their cronies, and this came to be the most dominant people in Ogoni. Thus, members of KAGOTE were able to exercise influence over appointments into government positions and the awarding of contracts, but in whose interests?

Writing on this development, Mr S.F. Nwika makes the point clear with regard to the political dispensation after the 1979 elections or what some others prefer to call the Second Republic, when he notes:

> The last three years have been a period marked by private prosperity in the midst of public poverty for the Ogoni people. While a few individual Ogoni leaders have done exceptionally well for themselves and their families within the present political system, the nationality is probably worse off today than under military rule.

He concludes:

> Our present-day leadership is prone to confuse personal with group interest. This weakens the moral base of leadership. It is my strongly held view that the problem of the Ogoni nationality in

the Second Republic can be placed at the door of our leaders. Most of our leaders faced for the first time by contracts with enormous wealth, have forgotten their bearing and their people.

This statement was made in 1982. Has the situation changed? No. Faced with the challenges of development and the implications this has for their legitimacy, Ogoni leaders formed the Movement for the Survival of the Ogoni People (MOSOP) in 1990. Shortly after its formation, however, there emerged a struggle for power within the organisation over leadership positions and access to power and resources. This soon led to cracks between a faction that was pro-government and another faction that lacked access to government and was thus radical. The struggle between the two groups led to the serious political crises which culminated in the murder of some moderate chiefs and leaders and the eventual execution of Saro-Wiwa and others by the government after a flawed trial by a military tribunal in 1995.

After the restoration of the democratic order in 1999, this scenario was to replay itself with those who called themselves representatives in government and the remnant elements within the Movement for the Survival of Ogoni People. This struggle undermines the hopes and expectations which the people had with the restoration of democratic government in Nigeria. For a people who have long been deprived, neglected, and exploited, the expectation was that democratic governance would lead to an improvement in living standards and increased access to resources and opportunities for the longevity of all. The opposite appears to be the case. While their leaders live in opulence, the vast majority of the people increasingly lapse into despair. The expectation has been raised with the visit of President Olusegun Obasanjo and Vice-President Atiku Abubakar to

Ogoni on separate occasions within the first two years of their assumption of office, when each of them was given a chieftaincy title.

The administration accordingly appointed prominent sons and daughters of Ogoni into positions of authority. Yet the majority of the people lived in squalor and destitution. In spite of this paradox, the Ogoni people in government listed the following as achievements of the Obasanjo presidency in a press release issued on the 14 May 2007, the departure period of the administration.

1. A visit by the President of the Federal Republic of Nigeria to Ogoniland on May, 2007. During that visit, the President laid the foundation stone for the monument of the Ogoni heroes, marking for the first time a concrete expression of the evil of internal hostilities within Ogoniland. The symbolism of this event was not lost on the Ogoni people in particular and the nation in general.

2. Resettlement of the families of the Ogoni 13.

3. Incorporation of more Ogoni into the federal and state governments.

4. A visit by a delegation of nearly 100 Ogoni people spread across the length and breadth of Ogoniland to meet with the President in Abuja.

5. Getting the United Nations Environment Programme (UNEP) to undertake the assessment study and subsequent clean-up of Ogoniland.

It is yet to be ascertained how these have resulted in the improvement of the vast majority of Ogoni people. The opportunities that could have improved the situation only end up being abused by the leadership. For instance, the creation of local government councils was expected to result in the improvement of the living conditions of the vast majority of the rural people. In Ogoni, these council areas are administered by Ogoni people themselves. Contracts were also awarded. The major contractors were Ogoni sons and daughters. Yet the contracts are never executed according to specifications, and many are abandoned after contractors may have collected mobilisation fees from government.

Between 1999 and 2010, vast resources have been allocated to local government councils. In monetary terms, these run into hundreds of millions of naira in the Ogoni area. What has happened to so much money? It has ended up as the private resources of council administrators, with the result that rather than development, Ogoni is degenerating into an under-developing society in which all indices of development are disappearing.

What Can Be Done?

The condition in Ogoni is degenerating, and if this is not addressed quickly, the experience of the recent past may be re-enacted on a grand scale. If people are deprived for too long, they tend to be frustrated, and such frustration only leads to aggression and violence. Ogoni needs a new kind of leadership. This is the leadership that is derived from the people and shares their values and aspirations. The current kind of leadership in Ogoni does not possess these attributes. For the new kind of leadership to emerge, the basic traditional structures and institutions of the community must be re-established and strengthened, and the local people must be empowered sufficiently. These structures and institutions are necessary to galvanise the people to believe once more in themselves and mobilise for development.

The lack of power for the community has meant that the authority of the people has been usurped by elites, motivated more by personal aggrandisement than by service to the community. The empowerment of the community implies a redefinition of the process of local governance. The leadership must first emerge from the family to the compound (*be*). From this, leaders will be recruited into the lineage councils, and from this leaders will be recruited into the town or village councils (*buan*). From village councils, an electoral college of village representatives should be established to produce leaders for the local government councils. The process of recruiting leaders based on partisan affiliations robs the people of their power to take decisions that affect them and to control those in positions of authority. Such leaders tend to owe their loyalty to their political parties and patrons within the party more than to the people. Thus, offices and positions are seen more as fiefdoms to be exploited for the benefit of both local leaders and their patrons. This must be addressed. More than that, there is the need for Ogoni people to convoke a nationality conference based on the representation of village and community councils. Such a conference is imperative in the evolution of a new kind of leadership for the people including decisions on the mechanism for community governance.

REFERENCES

Robert N. Lussier (2002) *Human Relations in Organisation: Application and Skill Building.* Fifth Edition. (Boston: MacGraw-Hill & Irwin).

Paul D. Sweeney and Dean B. MacFarlin (2002) *Organisational Behaviour: Solution for Management.* (Boston: MacGraw-Hill & Irwin).

Derek Torrington and John Chapman (1979) *Personnel Management.* (New Jersey: Prentice-Hall International).

Ogonis in Government, Draft Press Statement to MOSOP, 14 May 2007.

Eghosa, Osaghe "The Ogoni Uprising and Oil Politics: Minority Agitation and the Future of the Nigerian State".

Kenneth, M.C. Robert "Internal Colonialism: The case of Quebec." *Ethnic and Racial Studies*, Vol. 2, No. 3, July 1979.

Naanen, B. "Nigeria: Ogoni, an endangered indigenous people." *Indigenous Affairs*, April, June, 1995.

Naanen, B. "History, Politics and the Niger Delta: A reply to Bala Usman" *'Kiabara', Journal of Humanities*, Vol. 9, No. 1, 2003.

Naanen, B. Appendix A. "Progress of the Ogoni in Nigeria towards the attainment of International Development Targets (IDIs) for Poverty, Education and Health" in Richard Bourne, *Invisible lives under-counted, under-represented and underneath: The Socio-economic plight of indigenous people in the Commonwealth*. CPS Unit, May 2003.

Nwika, S. I. (1982) "This is not our Finest Hour" Keynote Address at the General Meeting of Ogoni Nationality held at Bori on Saturday 15 May 1982.

The Ogoni Union. *Constitution, Rules and Regulations*.

Saro-Wiwa (1995) *A Month and A Day: A Detention Diary*. (Ibadan: Spectrum Books).

Wolpe Harold (1975) "The Theory of Internal Colonialism: The South African Case" in Iror Oxaal, Tony Barnett, and David Booth (eds.) *Beyond the Sociology of Development: Economy and Society in Latin America*. Routledge and Kegan Paul.

Nna, N. J. (1999) *Oil and the National Question in Nigeria: The Niger Delta Experience*, Ph.D Dissertation, Uniport.

A. A. Jalloh "Neo-colonialism and the Prospects for Development in Africa" in <u>*The African* </u>*Review*, Vol. 11, No. 2, 1984.

Lemay, C. Michael (2002) *Public Administration: Clashing Values in the Administration of Public Policy*, Wadsworth Thompson Learning, U.S.A.